WINNING THE SALARY GAME:
Salary Negotiation for Women

WINNING THE SALARY GAME:
Salary Negotiation for Women

by

Sherry Chastain

John Wiley & Sons, Inc.
New York • Chichester • Brisbane • Toronto

Publisher: *Judy Wilson*
Editor: *Dianne Littwin/Gonnie Siegel*
Book production by *OT Productions*
  Production/Editorial Manager: *Rachel In*
  Designer: *Ronald. Misiur*

Library of Congress Cataloging in Publication Data

Chastain, Sherry, 1945-
  Winning the salary game.

  (Educational trade series)
  Bibliography: p.
  Includes index.
  1. Wages--Women--United States. 2. Negotiation.
I. Title. II. Series.
HD6061.2.U6C47   650.1'2   80-20622
ISBN 0-471-08433-6
ISBN 0-471-08023-3 (pbk.)

Printed in the United States of America
  81 10 9 8 7 6 5 4 3 2

To Mother, Gary and Nicholas

What This Book Is About

Do you believe that if you work hard on your job, you will be justly rewarded? If you do, look around. Women as a group still are earning only 59 cents for every dollar earned by men. Although the Women's Movement has overcome many job and pay barriers with the mandates of Title VII and the Equal Pay Act, it is still too frequently a game of "one-on-one" between a woman and her employer that determines whether she receives a fair return on her abilities and job performance. To get that fair return, you need to know how to negotiate. By negotiating, women stop discriminating against themselves and increase their earnings in the process.

Although you may not be negotiating with employers, they are always negotiating with you—for the lowest possible rate they can get away with. If you aren't negotiating, you just make their objective that much easier to attain. Whenever employers have the chance, they will depend on women's tendency to settle for less--or perhaps not to "settle" at all, but merely to acquiesce. For your part, if you don't know your own bargaining power, you may assume that you must accept the first figure that comes up in a negotiation or else decline the job. This assumption can be costly to you in lost earnings, but it is costly in another way. If you don't show some awareness of self interests by negotiating, employers are likely to conclude you aren't much of a bargain at any price.

Pay differentials between men and women, caused primarily by the clustering of women in low-paying positions, where 78 percent of all working women are found, will not disappear because women learn how to negotiate. But negotiating is a tool that women can use to improve their financial standing. A pay specialist at the Equal Employment Opportunity Commission partially attributes the poor showing in earnings of women to a general acceptance that salaries are not negotiable. On the other hand, some employers say women don't have the confidence to demand the price they are worth. Both assessments are correct. Perhaps by reading this book, you will gain greater self-confidence as you recognize that negotiating is necessary and as you acquire the skills to negotiate that this book provides.

I undertook the research and writing of this book not because I was a good negotiator but because I was a lousy negotiator. I thought it was solely my problem until I came to realize more and more that it was a common problem shared by most women and many men. Making effective demands for yourself without having them sounding like demands is hard work. Using my skills as a journalist, I set about finding some answers by extensively interviewing negotiating instructors, personnel directors, line managers, executive recruiters, management consultants, psychologists, career consultants, sales and marketing executives, government officials, compensation analysts, imagemakers, negotiating attorneys, women at the top, and women on the way up. I found answers for myself and some for you too.

SHERRY CHASTAIN

✠ ACKNOWLEDGMENTS ✠

Using my training and experience as a journalist, I went to hundreds of sources for data, input, and advice. For those who so graciously helped in the compilation of this book, I am deeply grateful. Among the direct and indirect contributors to the text are: Gonnie Siegel, Dianne Littwin, Ralph Minker, Sandra O'Connell, Connie Davis and Patrick McKoen (who assisted in researching the reference chapter), Fran Larkin, Max Hughes, Edward Grefe, Thomas Saltonstall, Ben Burdetsky, Virginia Kerr, Gary Chastain, Martha Jewett, Patsy Fryman, Richard Lathrop, Richard Irish, John Crystal, Hal Shook, Marilyn Shook, Bill O'Keefe, John Gordy, Jr., Dick McMullen, Bill Jaffe, Betsy Wade, Ann Nelson, Joyce Miller, Paula Bernstein, Stan Berk, Carole Cooper, Ann Buchwald, Diane Nicholson, Nancy Ames Thompson, Barbara Blaes, Gail Hughes, Carl Jacobs, Rosemary Storey, Carol Pitts, Anne Turpeau, Diane Armstrong, Johari Rashad, Elda Inoue, Jane Bachner, Ginger Levin, Kristine Marcy, Norma Loeser, Richard Brengel, Lisa Portman, Hannah J. Rayl, Nancy Wright, Esther Lawton, Trisha Fleetwood, Heidi Hoffman, Trudy Bryan, Eva June, Bill Devries, Jeff Manditch Prottas, Richard Womack, Cynthia McCaughan, Vickie Pierce, Jerry Penno, Robert Finley, Dee Rush, Nancy Russo, Gloria Harris, Donna Foster, Helen Lewis, Joyce Kennedy, Kathy Bowers, Geraldine Barfield, Bev Jackson, Mel Kampmann, Joel Albert, Mary Bloomfield, Frank de la Fe, Garylee Cox, Barbara Boyes, and many others including some who asked for confidentiality.

~ CONTENTS ~

WINNING THE SALARY GAME:
Salary Negotiation for Women

ONE

On Becoming A Negotiator

Most women—and many men—cannot talk about money. Perhaps money talk embarrasses us because our culture dictates that women are not supposed to ask questions about money or know about money. The extent of our embarrassment was captured in a letter "Dear Abby" received from a young woman complaining about the high cost of birth control pills. She believed her boyfriend should be sharing the expense, but she didn't think she knew him well enough to talk about money!

Financial knowledge conflicts with the perceived feminine characteristics of a "lady," in part because being a lady has meant being supported by a man. Although the number of women in the workforce is increasing and the number of single-paycheck marriages is decreasing, women working for cash, or having to, still may seem offensive or even vulgar to our traditional values.

Negotiator versus Nonnegotiator

When Mike Wallace of *60 Minutes* asked Johnny Carson how much money he was earning, the response was that people didn't talk about things like that in Nebraska. It is true that Carson would not discuss such matters publicly in Nebraska or anywhere else, but you can be sure that he or his representative has done some heavy money talking somewhere along the way. NBC would not pay him as high a salary as he receives unless he had made strong demands in tough negotiations.

Nonnegotiators avoid discussing money even at the appropriate time and place, often making a conscious effort to severely limit conversation on the subject. In the job interviewing process, I can remember going through lengthy sessions on work-related duties and responsibilities of little or no consequence in the long run and then spending only moments with an employer to determine my salary. I've since found that women do this all the time. Once I accepted a three-month assignment without even knowing what my salary would be (those nonnegotiating days are over now)! Vacationing in Europe on a long-awaited trip at the time, I was promised that my rewards would be "great" when I started the assignment, one that came, I might add, from a former employer.

Upon receiving my first check, I thought it seemed low for a week's work only to find out that the check was not for one week, but two. What I lacked in negotiating prowess at the onset of this job I quickly made up for with a show of independence. I returned the check to the employer, calmly but firmly telling him the salary was unacceptable. I shouldered my share of the blame for our mutual lack of communications on agreeing to this "great" salary and indicated the salary would have to be tripled for me to continue with the assignment of handling radio and television in a statewide political campaign. Fortunately, I had a powerful negotiating tool on my side which my employer, a campaign manager, did not have—time. Election day was rapidly approaching, and it waits for no one. He just didn't have enough time to spend looking for my replacement.

I listened to the usual objections you might expect to hear—I would be earning more than people who had been on the staff longer, for example—but my favorite argument was a variation on this political classic. My low salary was justified by claiming I was working on this campaign to promote better government. I was to think of my reduced salary as a contribution to that end. Good grief! I wouldn't budge. Finally, when the salary tripled, I stayed. The point of this story is that you can't expect your standard of fairness to mesh with someone else's, and justice will not prevail without your help. Despite my seeming victory, however, I still don't think our transaction had the elements of a successful negotiation, as I'll explain later.

The Link Between Taking Risks and Self-Esteem

I told this story to one woman who said, "That's fine for you to do, but I have two children who have a bad habit of wanting to eat three times a day. I can't take those risks!" Another woman said, "Come on, level with us. You must have had a 'daddy' ready to pay your bills." I bristled. Some of us don't negotiate because we have children and feel we can't afford to take the risk of losing the job. Then there are others of us without children who don't negotiate because we can get by without the extra money. Many of us think of ourselves as "little people" who have severely limited control over our lives. Such thoughts are mental strappings resulting from a lifetime of holding ourselves in low esteem. Poor self-images are evident when women see negotiating as reckless risk taking.

Measuring risks is a personal matter and closely tied to how you feel about yourself. What one person may regard as daring would be dismissed as uneventful to another. People seem to fall generally into two categories: those who think about what they might lose by taking risks and those who think about what they might gain. A chasm exists between the two types. Life for those in the first group at best becomes a matter of keeping things from getting worse. Those in the latter group, the risk takers, concentrate on how to make life better for themselves. The risk takers believe they are worth more, have higher aspirations, and usually end up with more of life's rewards. After generations of deferring, it is difficult for many women to muster the self-confidence to put themselves in the risk-taking category.

The question I hear frequently at speaking engagements is, with the economy bad and children to support what can we do to make more money without risking our jobs? I offer many question-asking and communication techniques among others throughout this book to help you calculate and minimize risks. But nobody can be assured of a cushion against the possibility of failure. You could lose the negotiation but you're not likely to lose your job if you've conducted yourself in a professional manner. On the other hand, you could lose a job regardless of whether you negotiate. Most things in life are not certain, so why not take risks? Granted, the state of the economy with mushrooming inflation and unemployment is a formidable factor, but if you have found yourself using this factor throughout most of your life as a reason for not taking risks, then perhaps you need to face up to another reason. Your thoughts may be trained on what you might lose rather than on what you might gain by taking a risk. While the economy, children, or limited education could reduce our options, these circumstances should not immobilize us to the point where we begin measuring risks out of fear instead of faith in ourselves.

As a reporter, I covered the campaigns of two congressmen who were in an extremely close primary race for the U.S. Senate. Both men were about the same age, both well-to-do, and both had two children. One, a self-made man, heavily committed his own personal funds to his campaign, an action which the other candidate was critical of. "What kind of person would jeopardize the financial security of his children on a campaign?" he asked, announcing he was not going to do that, although he had the money to do so. My first thought was that the second man was a truly selfless man, foregoing his own interests for the sake of his children. My second thought, the one that stuck, was he was thinking not about his children but about losing. And lose he did.

Many women, too, are guilty of this—they like to play the magnanimous victim, the sacrificial lamb, so that others will be happy and fulfilled. This lofty stance makes it easy to avoid taking risks or to fully commit yourself to success. Single-paycheck women with children who negotiate are saying that they have enough confidence in themselves that they will succeed and thereby be able to better provide for their families. The great success stories of all times have come from people with very little who were willing to put all they had on the line with the expectations of improving their lot in life. These people weren't thinking they had so few resources that they should do everything possible not to risk losing what they had. They were thinking that they didn't have all that much to lose anyway in light of what they might gain and besides, they were meant for bigger and better things!

Low self-esteem can keep you in low-paying jobs and low-paying jobs can keep your self-esteem low. If you think you are "little" and ineffectual, then you are. Ultimately, we determine our value to a certain extent in our respective fields. Those who have higher aspirations and those who think they are worth more will do better in negotiations on money. If you feel you are a worthwhile individual and you value your skills and yourself, then you will be willing to raise your aspirations and risk a particular job. Only you can measure the risk, but remember that security is in the mind alone and half the battle is realizing that you are a person of worth.

Accepting Criticism

Willingness to take more risks is only one aspect of negotiating. Women will have better luck at the negotiating table when they begin to view criticism in a different light. If your demands are challenged during negotiations (and they probably will be), take this as routine, not as a personal affront. Tell yourself it is only business. Receive criticism in an impersonal way and hear it as a positive way to improve. The less personal you are in your criticism of others, the less personal you will interpret criticism directed at you. It helps you and the process becomes more objective.

What Negotiation Is Not

Unfortunately, many of us tolerate salary inequities for years until we can no longer resist confrontation, erupting in anger with the ultimatum, "Raise my pay or I'm leaving!" This is the antithesis of negotiation, the ancient art built on accommodation, not confrontation. A successful negotiation is deliberate, not reactive, and should leave both parties with the feeling they have achieved something of value. In other words, the needs of both parties are considered and accommodated as much as possible. One party shouldn't feel that he or she has totally acquiesced or given in to the other person. My negotiation with the campaign manager had none of these qualities. It was a confrontation, not an accommodation. Convinced at the time that the guy must be riding through life on a loose saddle, I didn't try to learn his viewpoint. The negotiation was reactive, not deliberate and carefully thought out. I felt he was trying to take advantage of me and I reacted with an unusually high demand. He, on the other hand, felt I had held him up. The good will that should be present at the conclusion of every successful negotiation was not there.

Attitudes Toward Money

Another hindrance to women's development of negotiating skills is that many of us still feel it is in bad taste to ask for money for ourselves. This phenomenon is hooked to the Prince Charming syndrome to which many of us have fallen victim. We have grown up believing that we don't need to know about money matters because some extraordinarily handsome and competent man will handle those things for us. This myth denies present-day reality. The truth is that most men don't look, act, or earn the way a Prince Charming would. They may not know how to add up five Susan B. Anthony dollars; they can lose their jobs; they die before we do; and if that's not enough, the high incidence of divorce certainly breaks the heel off Cinderella's slipper. And for those who may have found a Prince Charming of sorts, is it really fair to expect somebody else to give us all the things we want in life? I think not.

Consequently, before we can grasp strategies and techniques of negotiation, we must examine our attitudes toward money and its importance in our society. Money, in and of itself, is not to be cherished, but it is to be recognized as a fact of life that money means survival. It can free you to live a creative life or the lack of it can condemn you to desperation. A 1974 study found that only money or affluence in America had a significant and positive effect on reports of "happiness." It was noted that "money talks, and our research suggests it also makes us happy."

For too long women have thought about coping instead of about making money. It would never occur to many of us to make money and pay somebody else to cope. Too frequently, we have thought about the minimum we will need to survive. But this is changing. It is delightful to hear more and more women today who say, "I want to get rich—earn millions" instead of the old volunteer image of giving all and getting nothing (at least not money) in return. One female executive I know has a plaque on her office wall which reads, "It doesn't matter whether you win or lose only how much money you make!"

The Yardstick of Success

In business, money is the yardstick others use to determine how well you are playing the game. The more chips you have, the better you're doing. The more you are paid, the more your company values you and the more other companies will value you. Even if you are one of those diehards who insists money is not all that important to you, there is a qualitative inference in what you are earning. If you are making $20,000 and someone else is doing the same thing for $23,000, it suggests that the other person is better than you are. That may not be true at all, but you are rated that way. If for no other reason than to be ranked fairly in your organization, you should be negotiating. In fact, if you aren't negotiating at the beginning of a job, you are missing the most important opportunity for fair treatment in the future. By settling for a rock-bottom salary floor, your future raises and benefits will be proportionately less. Over a career span of even ten years, your wage losses can be thousands of dollars.

TWO

Negotiating Basics

Employer versus Employee

Negotiating principles that can be applied between an employer and employee are timeless and universal. They can be applied whether you are a secretary or a chairman of the board. And the same objections we hear to our requests for a better salary have been heard through the centuries. One early account of a negotiation I came across in my research was ironically enough between two women. The story went something like this. Catherine II, the infamous Russian monarch, was treating her court to a series of performances by a talented ballerina of the day. The queen asked the ballerina what she expected to be paid for her performances and the dancer replied, "Five thousand gold coins." "Five thousand gold coins," exclaimed the queen. "That's outrageous. It is more than I pay my field marshals!" The ballerina retorted, "Perhaps your majesty should put one of the field marshals in a tutu!"

This woman was negotiating. She had named her price and wasn't backing down easily. Then as now, those who make high demands and hold out the longest do well in negotiations. Negotiators realize, too, that a natural adversary role exists between employers and employees. Employers are charged with keeping down costs, including your salary, and employees are or should be committed to getting fair compensation in exchange for services well-performed. Negotiators also understand that employers expect to negotiate with potential employees and that company budgets usually have some flexibility. Almost every salary is negotiable from a few dollars to many thousands.

Salary negotiations take place at the end of every successful job interviewing process. Negotiating is the natural culmination of that process. The interviewing stage may last one meeting, two, or several, but it does not end until you have a firm job offer or at least feel certain that you do. That is the appropriate time for the subject of money to be covered and the negotiating to begin. When individuals confer in an effort to arrive at a mutually beneficial agreement, they are negotiating. Therefore, at the root of all successful negotiating is effective communication. You are, in effect, teaching the employer why you are worth a higher salary and consequently you should know something about the way people learn. To reach your objective, your skills and accomplishments must be presented in a clear and organized way aimed at getting and holding attention. In the pages that follow, you will be introduced to broad principles of negotiating along with specific strategies and techniques.

Judgment and Timing

One quality common to all outstanding negotiators is judgment and timing. These I am calling one quality because one can't happen without the other. If you have good timing, then you have good judgment and conversely, if you have good judgment, then you have good timing. But if you've never negotiated effectively, or never negotiated at all for that matter, how do you get this seasoning? Going into a negotiation blind shows poor judgment right there. But if you go in knowing clearly what you want to achieve, being aware of strategies and techniques to help you get what you want, and, finally, not losing sight of your goals once in a negotiation, then your judgment has improved dramatically. Often in a negotiation we allow ourselves to get sidetracked on peripheral matters or we become so caught up in our side of the story that we forget what we really set out to do—to secure a higher income for ourselves. Naturally, our judgment and timing suffer. Thomas Saltonstall, a division director at the Equal Employment Opportunity Commission and a developer of negotiating classes in Washington, D. C., and Boston says, "It is important to be somewhat analytical in a negotiation and try to observe what you are doing in relation to what the other person is doing. It is very easy to get wrapped up in yourself." By heeding this, your judgment and timing in a negotiation can't help but be better honed.

However, the question of judgement and timing extends beyond the perimeters of the negotiation. It stretches, indeed, to how well you have prepared for the job you are seeking. A female corporate vice president told me, "Before you can exercise good judgment, you have to have information. One has to be up on her profession no matter which company you are in. It is a question of really being informed about the company's business and about how decisions are made. You have to build good contacts—informal contacts that cut across departmental and organizational lines. You have to stay tuned in and ask questions." Thus the acquisition of judgment and timing starts long before the negotiation itself.

Preparing and Rehearsing

Preparation, as you can readily see, is the first milestone to pass in the art of negotiating. Thorough preparation breeds confidence and reduces the chance of losing control in a negotiation. John Ilich,* a successful negotiator, says that "often during the course of preparation for the negotiation of large matters, I literally sit in the chair to be occupied by my opponent and mentally run through every one of my proposals in order to eliminate any flaws that may cause an unravelling as yarn in a knitted sweater will sometimes do."

To assess your level of preparation before negotiating, you'll need answers to several important questions that will be discussed in detail on subsequent pages. Questions such as what range is the employer likely to have established for this job? What will be your opening position? What is the lowest salary you would consider? What accomplishments in past job performances and educational

The Art and Skill of Successful Negotiation by John Ilich, Prentice-Hall Inc., Englewood Cliffs, N.J., 1973 Reprinted with permission.

attainments make you worth a higher salary? Why would the employer object to your opening price? Not enough experience? Budget won't permit it? Other employees aren't making that much? How would you answer those objections? Once you respond to the employer's objections, how might the employer counter your response? As you can see, it is not enough to anticipate questions in your preparation. You actually must rehearse answers.

Get a family member or a friend to role play with you. Rehearsing for a negotiation doesn't necessarily mean rote memorization of words, but rather having a firm grasp of all the issues. Figuring out how to emphasize your strengths and mask your weaknesses should help minimize any feelings of anxiety you might have once you are in a negotiation. Also, a carefully prepared oral sales presentation on yourself will not only convince the employer but provide him or her with information to convince others in the company's hiring process that you are a bargain even at a higher price.

Emphasize Accomplishments

Negotiations are future directed. You bargain for compensation in exchange for services yet to be performed. To do this, you should emphasize your accomplishments, not your personal needs. Employers don't care what you need. They care what they need. They want to determine how valuable you will be to the company, so speak in terms of your potential value by citing your accomplishments. It doesn't hurt to remind the employer that expenses will be greater should you accept this new offer or that you have two children nearing college age, which makes it imperative that you earn more. But again, the thrust of your pitch for a higher salary should be based on performance.

People tend to talk about what they have been doing on their last job and how they feel about what they have been doing instead of what they have accomplished in the past and what they want to accomplish in the future. Emphasizing accomplishments is not an exercise in raw egotism. Remember that the employer may need the information to convince others that you are a worthy candidate. You supply evidence that you are worth your asking price. Point out how you increased productivity and/or profits at your last place of work. For example, say "My sales for last year showed a 30 percent jump over the previous year." Or, if you are in clerical work trying to move to a higher-level job, you might say "I was an important member of a team that recorded a 20 percent increase in output over the past 12 months." If you are a fast copywriter in a business where deadlines are important, emphasize that you have never missed a deadline. If you work with numbers in a business where accuracy is paramount, underscore your habit of double-checking entries in order to avoid mistakes.

A negotiation is no place for undue modesty. It is the time for highlighting accomplishments. Most women fall behind in this because they often do not use effective terminology to describe their work experiences. Management consultant Bill Jaffe says that if women did an outstanding job of selling their expertise they would be helping themselves escape the handicap of compensation based on previous earnings, which is frequently on the low side. Use active words to describe your accomplishments: "I was responsible for . . ."; "I initiated . . ."; "I oversaw . . ."; "directed . . ."; "supervised . . ."; "took charge of . . . ." You can see how these words would be more effective than "I worked on . . .," "I did . . .," or "I assisted . . . ."

Give the employer time to absorb what you say. Your accomplishments are easier for the employer to grasp when time elapses between each one rather than when they are all grouped together. For best results, separate the descriptions of your strengths with questions directed at the employer. You can use this method to test the employer's understanding of each accomplishment before you go on to the next. Allow time for discussion so you will have an idea of how well you are communicating.

Think of the Other Person

People who enter negotiations are usually beset by thoughts of their limitations and shortcomings. After all, who knows them better? A good antidote is to concentrate on the employer's problems in relation to your negotiation. The first may be time pressure —desperation to get someone on the job immediately. Time is the principal factor in negotiations. In addition, keep in mind a variety of more subtle things about the employer. Your talents may enhance your employer in the eyes of higher-ups in the organization. Don't overlook the fact that the employer probably wants to complete the hiring process and be thought of as a fair and reasonable person as well. If you have made a high salary demand and have communicated sufficient accomplishments to back it up, your prospective employer may be rooting for you and making notes on how to sell you to the company.

Our perceptions and assumptions of others are also important. These factors have a definite effect on how we behave toward another person and, in turn, how that person responds or reacts to us. You should begin with the assumption that the employer is basically a friendly, sincere person. If you treat the employer accordingly, he or she will tend to be friendly and sincere to you. Don't wait and see what the employer's reaction to you is going to be. Take the first step yourself.

Identifying Needs

Your success in a negotiation depends largely on how well you assess your potential employer's needs and how well you communicate your accomplishments which best satisfy those needs. However, knowledge of what is important to the employer is not always easily uncovered. Management consultants Mack Hanan, James Cribbin, and Herman Heiser* have appropriately termed the other person's needs "proprietary possessions." In negotiating, you deal with needs on at least two levels. First, the company's needs. In determining what those needs are, it is best to look at a rival company's potential threat. The strength of the competition can define a company's underlying priorities. Perhaps a more compelling set of needs are those of the individual with whom you are negotiating. These needs should include the company's needs but they are more likely to in-

Consultative Selling by Mack Hanan, James Cribbin and Herman Heiser, Amacom, a division of American Management Association, Inc., New York, 1973. Reprinted with permission.

clude the desire for personal power, prestige, recognition, promotion, or money. The employer wants to know what there is about you that will help achieve what is most important to him or her. Sometimes a need can be surprisingly uncomplicated—perhaps simply wanting to conclude the negotiation. Many negotiations have been won solely because the other party wanted to be home at a certain time and did what had to be done to wrap it up!

To accurately perceive the needs of the employer, you should also examine how others may perceive you. Might your personal makeup impede your ability to recognize the needs of the other person? For example, do you interrupt instead of hearing a person out? Test yourself to see if you are guilty of "selective inattention," that is, listening only to those things that you want to hear and tuning out all the rest. What quirks do you have that may divert attention away from your abilities? Poor eye contact could suggest a demeanor that may or may not be true about you. It could indicate that you are a shy person, but it could also indicate that you are not to be trusted. Another consideration to keep in mind as you find out the other person's needs is to disagree agreeably. Let the employer know that you are disapproving only of an idea and not his or her personality, character, or intelligence. (Communication tips will be covered later.) Attention to details like those just discussed will help you identify what is really important to the other person. Not until you make this identification can you realistically expect to meet and satisfy the employer's needs, thus justifying your asking price.

Asking Questions

Of course, the art of asking questions is paramount in pinpointing the other person's priorities so you can sell your ability to meet them. Some of the most useful questions to help uncover needs are—Why? What do you mean? What happened when . . .? What would happen if . . .? How do you feel about it? What do you think? Why is it done that way?

The great value of asking questions is that it enables you to learn more, to set up a better climate for the exchange of ideas and create conditions for understanding and commitment that will be to your advantage. People fail to probe all the time. For instance, an employer might say to you, "We can't do that!" Simply ask a gently probing question that shows interest in the company and allows the employer an opportunity to think. You would ask something like, "It seems plausible to me. Is there a special reason you can't do it?" It can be said that those who develop into good negotiators are those who are prepared to ask intelligent and well-timed questions.

Learn to Listen

It will do little good to ask questions if you don't listen to the answers. A major psychological advantage can be gained by the person who really knows how to listen. It is immensely satisfying to the other person to know that his/her viewpoint is thoroughly understood and given due weight. Many fail to master the art of listening because they are thinking of what they will say next instead of giving full attention to the person who is talking. So relax and listen carefully and patiently to what the employer stresses. Then you can stress the same kinds of things as you build your case for higher earnings.

Be aware too of the importance of the unspoken word as well as the spoken word. By listening "between the lines" you may discover parts of questions that the employer is avoiding, which may have significance in your particular negotiation. Also listen to the tone of voice, emphasis, and repetition, all of which can change the nuance of a word. Observe body language, including facial expressions, gestures, and fidgeting. "Listening," according to management consultants Hanan, Cribbin, and Heiser, "is accomplished by the eye as well as the ear. The language of motion and the language of emotion in addition to the language of words are equally important avenues of communications."

The average person retains about half of what he or she has just heard. This isn't good enough for a successful negotiator. Listening is one of the ways you will uncover the real concerns of the employer. If you do not uncover those needs, you won't have a chance to demonstrate how you can meet them, and success at the negotiating table will elude you.

Another element of good listening is to withhold judgments and decisions until after the other person has finished talking. If you make up your mind to listen to ideas that might weaken your argument for higher earnings as well as those that might strengthen your case, you are in little danger of missing what people have to say. A method you can use to test how fully you are grasping what is being said to you is the confirmation process. At each step of the way, actually confirm what you believe you have learned. After the employer has expounded on an idea, you might say, "If I've understood you correctly, you are saying . . . ." This technique helps you protect yourself against the perils of your own "selective inattention" and it also reassures the other party that you do indeed understand his/her point of view.

When you listen, you enter the other person's world and comprehend a frame of reference other than your own. With good listeners, the person talking will open up and say more clearly what is on his or her mind. With poor listeners, the person talking sometimes withdraws partially and does not say exactly what he or she feels. Listening, you see, is hard to resist. When you listen to me, I become obligated to listen to you.

THREE

More Fundamentals of Negotiating

Building Trust

If the negotiator has consciously built a feeling of trust during the interviewing process, it will provide immense latitude when the discussion turns to salary. An initial impression of calmness and deliberation will carry over and make the employer more receptive throughout the negotiation. You can establish the kind of rapport that will produce beneficial negotiating results by utilizing the principles already covered: preparing and rehearsing, emphasizing accomplishments rather than personal needs, ascertaining the needs of the other person, asking intelligent questions, and carefully listening. If you can consciously incorporate these basic negotiating elements into your professional style, your stature is bound to grow in the eyes of the employer.

Another way to build trust during the interviewing process is to start each discussion on common-ground issues. When you emphasize similarities rather than differences, the likelihood that the employer will accept your goal is improved. This may entail small talk for a few seconds on relatively minor matters or perhaps matters that have no direct connection with the issue to be negotiated. Your purpose is to work toward a common ground and anything that will assist in this is good. When you, as a negotiator, share a similar experience with the employer, don't be reluctant to recall it. Perhaps you have the same hometown. Remember, you are trying to persuade. Persuasion begins when you show respect for the other person's ideas no matter how different they are from yours. We do not have to agree with all the ideas and opinions of others, but we are required to try to understand a viewpoint other than our own and realize that we might have come to the same conclusions had we been sitting on the other side of the desk.

Say It Again . . . and Again

Use repetition as a negotiating tool to sell your expertise. Since no one can absorb everything that is said, repeat and repeat. The importance of repetition is well-illustrated in the old advertising adage: Tell them what you are going to tell them, tell them, and then tell them what you've told them. Use repetition to reemphasize accomplishments and significant points, to refresh the employer's memory, and to clarify information.

One way to repeat ideas without monotony is to use examples. An example is nothing more than an idea reduced to a specific case. Another way to avoid tedious repetition is to use synonyms for key words. For instance, one time you might say, "I direct . . ." and the next time you could say, "I oversee . . . ." Still another technique is to enlarge on a basic idea by adding a bit more information to it each time it's repeated. To illustrate this, a person who produces a television news program might say, "I produce a news program which jumped 20 percent in ratings this year." Always threading the profit-oriented idea of ratings in your presentation, you might next say, "I attribute the large increase of viewers from 18 to 49 years old to four factors. First of all, our audience started to climb when we broke three major local stories in succession . . . ." This person has repeated the ratings accomplishment three different times in three different ways in three different but successive sentences. And each time it is repeated, a little more information is added.

Silence Is Golden

Short, strategically placed periods of silence are valuable, because they allow both parties to think for a few seconds. Silence also gives time for evaluation. But silence has another highly important use in negotiating. California-based career consultant Eli Djeddah* maintains that if you deliberately impose a silence, the other person will break it within 30 seconds. This can be very useful when you discuss money. For example, if the employer names the salary figure first, all you have to do is repeat the number, look dismayed, and cast your eyes toward the floor—in silence. By consciously initiating the silence and sticking to it, odds are the employer is likely to come back with a better offer, or at least encourage further negotiating in less than 30 seconds.

One woman used this tactic quite unknowingly when the employer quoted her a salary much higher than she had expected to get. Dumbstruck, she just sat there staring at him, in silence. The employer, mistaking her reaction as a rejection of his offer, then came back with an even higher offer. Silence has its golden rewards.

Know Your Worth

A cornerstone of successful negotiating lies in knowing what your skills are worth on the job market. Even more specifically, the implementation of successful negotiating strategies is aligned with knowing what range the employer is thinking about paying for the job you're considering. While salary research was touched on as an important component of preparing for a negotiation, the subject is special enough to be developed within its own parameters.

The main thrust of your market research is to determine a realistic range that the employer is likely to have in mind for the job. You have to think in terms of a range. People, jobs, and economic situations have too many variables for an employer to say this position is worth exactly $19,374.32, and it would be next to impossible for you to pinpoint a figure that closely in your survey of the market. Understanding that competitive employers have to maintain competitive salaries, you need to remember also that some employers may put more value on a set of skills than others. How accurately you

---

Moving Up, by Eli Djeddah, Ten Speed Press, Berkeley, Calif., 1978. Reprinted with permission.

assess the employer's range becomes the foundation for executing successful negotiating strategies that are addressed in the next chapter. If you rely on the employer to tell you what your skills are worth on the job market, you aren't negotiating. He/she is there to pay as little as possible for your services.

You bargain from a position of strength when you know your salary expectations are based on a rational, objective study of the market. By knowing your market worth, you won't back down quite so easily when the employer challenges your demands. Of course, your market value has nothing to do with your worth as a valuable human being on which no dollar amount can be established, but on the job market, you can place a price on your head, though not without effort.

More on Market Knowledge

Unquestionably, there are those who have unrealistic notions of their value. As one manager told his employee, "I'll pay you what you're worth, but I hate to see you starve to death." A serious problem among women, though, is that they undervalue their own skills and, even more acute, many simply don't know what the market will bear. "I didn't know what to say so I named eight dollars an hour," recalls Fran Williford, an executive secretary, when the employer asked her about salary requirements. Cheryl Harper, who was about to begin using her economic background in a law firm after being out of the labor market for several years, recalls saying to her employer, "My husband thinks [this answer suggests that she can't think for herself] I should be getting $20,000 a year." Fortunately for these two women, however, their lack of knowledge about their market value did not penalize them as it does many women because their figures happened to be on the high side of the going rates for their skills. "Those who research the market and know the going rates usually end up with higher salaries," says Bill O'Keefe, formerly the director of management and budget and now vice president for the American Petroleum Institute. He believes women tend to have less information about the market than men.

An executive recruiter I interviewed says knowledge about your market worth is an important aspect of projecting the right p.- fessional image. She says her more than fifteen years of experience suggest that women accept what is offered to them much more quickly than men. "The majority of women do not ask for a whole lot more than they are making now and often come across as indicating they would make a lateral move for the right opportunity, whereas men generally believe the opposite." This headhunter asserts that most men would expect a jump in earnings when they change jobs and they are not inclined to create the impression that they would come aboard without added compensation. Management consultant Bill Jaffe says women come in at the lower end of the range for two reasons. First, their actual pay may be suppressed and second, they may not know their market value. "We have people who come in here," says Jaffe, "and they don't have the foggiest idea as to what the marketplace commands."

Sources for Salary Data

Although most major companies conduct annual salary surveys, they often squirrel them away from public scrutiny. Even the Equal Employment Opportunity Commission often has to resort to subpoenas to get information on salaries in various companies. This helps explain how a man and a woman can work side by side at equal jobs for years before the woman discovers she is being paid less. Many companies are accused of keeping the rates secret in order to avoid the sizable cost of restructuring a pay system. While some companies are particularly adamant about the confidentiality of salary ranges, others are a little more open. If you are trying to determine your market worth, you have nothing to lose by calling a company that employs people with your skills and experience to inquire about salary ranges. Admittedly, it is a long shot that you will get the information you want. Try calling a company's personnel office and ask to speak to a person in wage and salary administration. If the person is receptive to your request, ask also how their salaries for your job compare to other salaries in the industry. Are they on the high side or the low side? As mentioned, some salaries for identical jobs can vary widely within the same industry mainly because one company may place more value on those skills than another. And, too, jobs with similar titles can be defined differently from one company to the next. Companies frequently give these reasons for not wanting to reveal salary ranges.

One ready source of salary information is classified ads in newspapers. A look at pay scales in several want ads will help you begin to get a feel for your job value. Keep in mind that ads are there to attract attention, so the salary you see by looking at only one ad may or may not be representative of the entire market. The best source of salary information, however, can be business and trade journals connected with your field. Libraries and colleges, both of which are gold mines for salary information, subscribe to a large number of these publications. These magazines regularly publish articles on earnings in addition to carrying classified sections where further salary data appear in want ads. Also, several public and private salary surveys often can be found in libraries, college placement offices, and individual schools within a college system. The negotiating references section in the back of this book has detailed information on what you can expect to find on salaries in libraries and on college campuses.

You should use several sources to be sure you have an accurate account of what the market will bear for one with your skills. For women, an important and growing channel for pay data is other women in network organizations and support groups. These resources can help you identify, for example, a sympathetic woman in a personnel department who, in turn, can help you get the salary information you need. As time goes on, these grapevines will prove to be even more beneficial.

Executive recruiters and employment agencies (public and private) are other sources for salary data. If you are currently earning from $20,000 to $25,000 and up, you should look to executive recruiters for possible assistance. Below that, try employment agencies. One headhunter told me you have a fifty-fifty chance of getting the information you want when you make a cold call to a search firm. It stands to reason that if you catch someone on a busy day, it may affect your odds for success. When you call, ask to speak to a recruiter who has experience in your field. If no one does, ask to be directed to executive recruiters who do have knowledge of your industry.

You might want to consider calling the national business or trade association for your line of work. A directory of associations in your local library will assist you in locating an address and a phone number (see the Negotiating References Section). Several associations have placement divisions charged with keeping current salary information. If you do use national data in trying to determine your market worth, you will need to inquire how much of an adjustment is necessary for the salary range to accurately reflect the region in which you live. And another reminder. Check to see how old the salary data are no matter which sources you use. If the data are more than a year old, which they probably will be, allow for an annual cost-of-living increase of 8 percent.

Setting Your Own Range

Once you've done your research and feel confident that you know what range the employer probably expects to pay for the job in question, you need to set some salary boundaries of your own. First of all, you will want to decide what your opening position will be. That number has to be higher than you realistically expect to get but, nevertheless, one you can justify. You are giving yourself room to negotiate, and that basic negotiating strategy will be fully discussed in the next chapter. Many women hurt themselves by naming too low a figure for their opening position if they know enough to name one at all. On the whole, women seem to have lower aspirations than men. The key to higher negotiating rewards is through higher aspirations. If you don't negotiate for more, then your only alternative is to settle for less. Raise your aspirations. The second number you need to fix is your bottom line—the lowest dollar figure you will consider for the job. That bottom line number is what the employer is searching to find from his or her side of the desk. If you are negotiating, it is not likely to ever be discovered.

FOUR

Strategies and Techniques of Negotiating

Delay Money Talk

Pfizer divisional vice president Max Hughes says it is "dumb" for a job candidate to raise the question of salary early in the hiring process. And it is. Until the employer has had time to make up his or her mind to hire you, you aren't worth anything to the employer. St. Louis sales executive Robert Finley said, "I've had people come in here and proceed to tell me what all their requirements are. I know they are out. I don't really care what their requirements are at that stage of the interview!" Remember that when you negotiate you should listen and ask questions in order to identify the other person's needs and then communicate how you can help meet them. You should show how you will make life easier—not more difficult—for the employer and how your services can contribute to his/her future well being. By delaying the subject of salary until later in the process, you can raise your worth in the employer's eyes. Loaded with information about your strengths, the employer can see you as a more valuable asset than you were in the beginning.

If the employer raises the question of money early in the process— before a job offer has been made to you—say, "It has been my guide-line not to talk about salary unless I'm asked to consider a definite position. I'm sure you understand. Right now, I'd like to know more about your company and departmental goals and how my role would fit into these objectives." Or simply say, "Before we get into a job offer and salary, tell me about your plans for this department and what contribution you would expect from me." This technique helps you pinpoint the attributes you possess that are important to the employer. If you listen carefully, you will know which of your qualifications to stress when it comes time to press for the salary you deserve.

Another reason for putting off the subject of money early in negotiations is "sunk time." An employer who has "sunk" or spent time interviewing you doesn't want to feel that the time was wasted. The hours in a business day are too important a resource to waste. You are in a stronger position to discuss money after postponing the subject because by now the employer may already see you as hired and go to greater lengths to accommodate you.

A third reason for delaying money talk is quite frankly that the harder people are to get, the more valued they are. Moreover, delaying shows you are interested not only in what you earn but in what you do. All around, your negotiating position is improved by not being too eager to raise the question of money.

When to Talk Money

When you are certain or relatively certain you have a concrete job offer, turn the discussion to compensation. If you aren't sure how serious the employer is about your candidacy, you might try this technique. Ask "What would be the advantages of leaving my present company and joining this organization?" One woman who asked this question said she knew she had the job as soon as the employer launched into a pitch on the superiority of his company.

Inevitably, the employer who wants you on his/her team will ask, "What are your salary requirements?" Unlike some career consultants who encourage you to get the employer to name the first figure, executive recruiter Richard Irish, career consultant John Crystal, job market analyst Richard Lathrop, and others say, and I agree, that you should name the first figure and you should make it high.

How High the Sky?

As mentioned, a fundamental strategy in the art of negotiating is to give yourself room to negotiate. When the Teamsters negotiate with management, they usually come out with an agreement close to their opening position. But they have muscle (through numbers) that most of us don't have. If we were to walk in and open with our bottom line figure, we'd come out wearing a barrel. So the rationale behind negotiating is always to open with a figure higher than you expect to get.

But how much is "high" and how much is "higher?" High is the top of the employer's range and, of course, higher is anything above that. So you can see how important it is to research the market. You may decide that 5 percent above the employer's range is higher, or 10 percent, or 20 percent. Your opening figure will be based on many factors, including how badly the employer wants you and how effective you are in convincing him/her that you are worth a good price. Thomas Saltonstall, a negotiating instructor, says you should ask 20 percent more than you expect to get. "If I had a fairly good sense of the amount they were thinking of paying, I would tend to ask for a figure 20 percent higher, which might bring an emotional reaction, but maybe a productive one."

The opening stages of a negotiation are usually an educational process. When you ask for a figure higher than is realistic, but one nevertheless that you can justify in rational terms, the response from the employer may be something like, "What you are asking for is 20 percent above my range! Are you out of your mind? I'll talk about increasing my range a bit but it won't be 20 percent!" At this point the employer is committed to talking about a salary range higher than he originally had in mind. Saltonstall says, "I'd immediately respond with, It's good to hear you say that the salary range is going to be increased and I hope we can agree on a figure that's satisfactory. Already you have them locked in. You've got them acknowledging that there is going to be a range increase."

Job market analyst Dick Lathrop* advises naming a figure 5 percent

Who's Hiring Who by Richard Lathrop, Ten Speed Press, Berkeley, Calif., 1977. Reprinted with permission.

higher than the top of the established pay range. When the employer balks as he/she quite naturally will, say "Then what is the best you can do for me in the way of my salary?" Lathrop says that the employer's impulse will be to put the rate as high as possible—maybe at the top of the range—because you obviously attach strong value to the quality of your work and certainly must have a reason for it. Some also do it just to keep from feeling cheap. But what if the employer still insists on a figure in the lower part of the range? Persevere. Say, "Could you possibly swing (naming a figure somewhere in the middle)?" You are entitled to top pay for your talents, and techniques like these will help you get what you are worth.

John Crystal, founder of the John C. Crystal Center for Creative Life/work Planning of Manhasset, New York, also recommends that your opening figure should be higher than the employer's range. He says, "You should have your range clearly in mind. If your research has been good enough, you know that the top of your range exceeds, to a limited extent, that which the other person has in mind."

Irish* too encourages you, as I do, to make it your business to find out what the employer intends to pay for the job before you begin salary negotiations. Then when you sense you have the job offer, you should name the top figure in the employer's range. He says, "Always establish what you want before the employer does. If the employer establishes a salary offer before you have staked your position, and the offer is considerably less than yours, your leverage is lost."

Whether you decide to make your gambit the top of the employer's range, 5 percent above it, or 10 or even 20 percent above it, the negotiating principle remains the same: open with a figure higher than you realistically expect to get. By giving yourself room to negotiate, you improve your chances for a better salary, which should make you happy. At the same time, you will make your employer happy because he/she has been able to bring you down from your opening position. Thus you will have had a successful negotiation: where the two parties believe they have benefited from the transaction, and

*Excerpts from *Go Hire Yourself an Employer* by Richard K. Irish. Copyright © 1972, 73, 78. Reprinted by permission of Doubleday & Company, Inc.

where not money but mutual satisfaction is exchanged.

If You Are Unsure of the Employer's Range

You'll get better results if you know the employer's range before you negotiate and then take the initiative to name a high figure first. This strategy causes the employer to think of you in higher terms than he/she might have otherwise. However, if you are not quite sure of yourself or the employer's range, you may prefer to let the employer be the one to start naming figures. While you will want to exercise as much control as possible during a negotiation, much of that control can come from listening carefully to what the other party says. The employer may use either a straightout manner on salary or a more indirect method. He/she may say something like "There is just a small detail left. What kind of salary requirement do you have?" If you are asked this, turn it back to the employer. Say, "I am enthused about the prospects we have discussed and I am sure a well-managed company like this has a fair range for this position. What is your range?" Always ask for a range. Don't allow yourself to get stuck on a specific figure which will make it more difficult to negotiate upward. Asking the employer for a range under these circumstances protects you from the biggest mistake possible in salary negotiations: naming too low a figure. A woman who is a data-processing manager in New York used this technique to her advantage. She inquired about the range and was surprised to learn it was much higher than she had dared to anticipate. Had she first named her figure, which was based on low aspirations, she would have lost several thousand dollars right off the bat. Remember, you can retreat from a high figure but you are not likely to recover from too low a pricetag.

As a note here, I realize that some of you will think I use outlandish figures in upcoming examples, and that my advice must apply only to an elite group of women. Not true. I have deliberately chosen higher figures for effect, not as cross-sectional earning patterns among women. We are frequently guilty of having low expectations. One way to raise our aspirations is to think of salaries in higher figures.

Once the employer names a range—let's say $19,000 to $23,000—
what do you do then? You look thoughtful and you say "Up to
$23,000?" Write it down on your note pad. At that point, be silent
and slowly count to thirty. It is not up to you to make it easy for
the employer. He or she has to bite the bullet and give you a figure.
While you are counting to yourself, the employer is caught and can
only evade the inevitable for a minute or two by talking about all the
fringe benefits. Management likes to emphasize the total financial
package by talking about the "extras"—health plan, pension or retirement systems, eligibility for insurance programs, parking, profit-
sharing plan, stock options, use of a car, credit cards, expense account, and so forth. But regardless of all this, the employer has to
give you a figure.

If the figure quoted to you is not high enough, say so. Reaffirm
your mutual interest and be straightforward. For example, say "I
need to be frank with you. I am interested in what we have been
talking about and I don't want to close any doors yet, but the figure
you just named is not an adequate incentive for me to join your team.
I do know that we are working within a range and we are both interested, so let's keep talking with one another."

The Unlikely Event

In the unlikely event that you negotiate a higher salary than others
already on the payroll who have similar responsibilities, don't expect
to be warmly welcomed into the fold. These things have a way of
leaking out. And Irish says, "Many will make it a point to see that
you 'fail' on the job." I saw this happen to a friend of mine in television news. She joined a staff at a salary much higher than others
were receiving and she was undermined from the very beginning. It
was a bewildering and bitter experience for her. In retrospect, she
might have been well-advised to negotiate a salary near the level of
long-term employees with the understanding that she would take a
financial stride up the ladder at the end of three months. By then,
she would have had a chance to make friends and establish herself.
The irony of the whole incident is that she had actually performed
an enormous favor for the other staff members. Her high salary

meant the negotiating floor for the others had been raised. Being nonnegotiators, they never saw or understood this.

Bargain Basement Mentality

Most of us think by not costing very much we will have a better chance at good jobs, but this is an erroneous notion. The worst thing in negotiations is to undervalue ourselves. If we put a small price on ourselves, that's about what the employer will think we are worth. Low aspirations can actually disqualify you from jobs.

The truth of this statement was brought home to me a few years ago. I was asked to find a speaking instructor to coach a congressional candidate in the midwest. After a search of several days, I found a person with excellent credentials to coach the candidate at a cost of $10 a session. I rushed to tell this to the campaign manager. He failed to share my enthusiasm and joked, "Who can have confidence in anybody who only costs $10?" There you have it. If that same speaking instructor had assessed her worth at $200 a session, she would have been hailed as the "Virtuoso of Verbiage." Her qualifications weren't the discrediting factor, but her price was. She had no idea what her skills were worth and it reflected negatively on her professionalism. Saltonstall discusses the question of value by saying, "You have to gently but assertively let somebody know that he/she should pay you what you are worth. If you don't do that, employers naturally come to the conclusion that you are worth what you are being paid."

Crystal says his experiences bear this out. "I let them see for themselves that they have been operating on a false premise (by not negotiating). Women, in particular, feel that sitting there or lowering their price will improve their chances for a job. This is a mistake. If you have got what that organization needs, it will bargain with you. Women have been taught that it is unladylike to bargain for themselves and they have to get over that. It makes them look weak, unbusinesslike, unrealistic and unprofessional." Dr. Gloria Harris, a behavioral psychologist, says she hears women in her management and assertiveness training classes voice the concern that they are afraid they will lose their femininity. She says she assures them that femininity is something you don't lose just because you go in and negotiate in an effective manner.

The Loyalty Factor

The basis of successful salary negotiating is being a good performer, knowing what your skills are worth on the market, and applying negotiating know-how to get the salary you deserve. Most women in the workforce are good performers who underestimate their worth. After three thousand years of being identified as less valuable than men, many women have difficulty commanding sufficient self-confidence to put a high price on themselves. On the other side of the coin, however, are a few women who try to put an expensive tag on themselves without a performance record to back it up. As one businesswoman told me, "Those few are frankly women who don't know very much about business. They think because it is women's time, they are going to waltz in and take the cake. Well, they aren't going to do it." It seems to me that kind of naivete among even a few would pass quickly. Anyone who works in a competitive environment knows the cake is hard to get even when you're carrying a bowl of icing.

A more widespread failing among women observed by Norma Loeser, the only woman to head a major business school in the country (George Washington University in Washington, D. C.) is that some women tend to say I like this job or this boss and therefore completely put themselves out of the marketplace. Then one day they find out they are making five thousand dollars less than they should be, but the discrepancy lies in the fact that they haven't actively sought other opportunities. Loeser says, "I have a philosophy that women aren't quite as capable of disconnecting themselves from an organization in a cold way. Their heart seems to be attached to the company." She cautions women not to get so attached to the organization that they misjudge their contribution. "Some think," she says, "that the organization can't get along without them. In fact, they might not necessarily be disappointed that you leave."

Another pragmatic argument against feeling undue loyalty toward a company was expressed by Saltonstall. "Some tend to put an awful lot of emphasis on being promoted within the organization. They are afraid to look around for better opportunities someplace else and that is a big mistake. If you are a real achiever, generally organizations are not capable of providing the kind of rapid career growth that you deserve. I would never have had the upward mobility that I have had if I had set my sights just within the organization where I was."

Some women continue to see themselves as office wives and mothers instead of job holders and they stay on jobs because they feel needed. Sacrifice is an ancient practice that ought to be stopped. Management consultant Gonnie Siegel says she advises women "to knock off this attitude. Keep moving up. There is not an infinite amount of time." Irish says to start looking for your next "gig" as soon as you land your current one and if you find a more desirable, higher paying job two months later, take it. "It's crackers to be obligated to employers."

How to Overcome Objections to Your Price

Expect objections to flow as soon as you have named your opening price. Among the most common objections raised by employers are our budget can't stand that, other employees aren't making that much, and it's a lot more than you've been making. (Suggested answers for these and other objections are upcoming.) When the employer is telling you why you are not worth your asking price, don't interrupt. Some take it personally when they are interrupted, but there is a better reason for hearing them out. While the employer is talking, you can't be giving anything away. As Jeffrey Manditch Prottas, who teaches a negotiating class at Harvard University, says, "You never lose the negotiation while the other person is talking." As long as you are not giving your consent, the employer can't make an agreement without you.

Be sure you don't give any nonverbal signals, though. As the employer speaks, resist the urge to nod your head up and down. As Prottas reminds us, "Shaking your head indicates that you are listening, but in the context of a negotiation, people may read that sign as an indication that you are agreeing with what they are saying." Instead of encouraging the other person to fully voice his/her position —as you want to do—your nodding may reinforce in the employer's mind the negative aspects of your candidacy and the inappropriateness of your demands.

After the other person has expressed his/her objection, you can use several techniques to effectively help you get around the obstacle in your path to higher earnings. You might try paraphrasing what the employer has said. This is important psychologically because it assures the employer that you have listened to his/her viewpoint and it shows that you understand what has been said to you. Because you have listened, appreciated, and taken into account the other person's point of view, that person should now be more inclined to do the same for you. It is not advisable to disagree immediately with an objection. Instead, you should ease into your reply. Either paraphrase what you have heard or say, "You have brought up an interesting point . . . ," but don't indicate that you agree with the employer's objection.

Perhaps an even better way to begin answering the employer's objection to your price is to rephrase his/her comments in such a way to evoke a "yes" answer. For example, "It is my understanding that you are concerned about . . . . Is that correct?" Then give your answer to the objection. You might conclude with another "yesable" question. "That's some accomplishment, isn't it?" Quite naturally, it is more difficult to move into a "yes" series when the employer raises a hard-to-handle objection. At this point, the main thing to do is not to agree with him/her. We are inclined to say something like "You are absolutely correct, but . . . ." As mentioned, when you respond this way you only reinforce the negatives already in the employer's mind. A better way to respond to an objection that is hard to overcome is to stress those accomplishments of yours which are most important to the employer.

The Female Handicap

Women have to be particularly careful in answering objections posed by some male employers. Dr. Gloria Harris, a behavioral psychologist, says "I think that many men, of course, feel threatened by competent women. One has to be sensitive to the fact that even though the norms in our culture are changing rapidly, there are still many individuals who are perhaps five or ten years behind the time and women just have to be aware of the different expectations of people." And some employers may feel less free in communicating their true concerns to a woman, particularly a black woman, because they feel what they say may be "illegal" in today's social climate. (Who knows, it may be!) If you sense this uncertainty and suspect what the underlying concern is, you might try volunteering information about yourself in order to deal with the unexpressed objection. For example, the employer might be hesitant to ask whether you have children whose care might interfere with travel plans connected with the job. However, don't assume his communication problems are yours. You may have to cope with them, but the problems remain clearly his.

As a side note here, negotiations can give you insights into the character of a company or an employer. While we want to be paid our market worth, money isn't the only factor in job satisfaction. Personal respect and fair company policies are two other factors. If you find yourself increasingly apprehensive about the employer's integrity at this late stage of the hiring process, you might want to reconsider your options. For instance, if an employer hints in the negotiations that you might inflate an expense account from time to time to help offset a less than desirable salary, you most definitely would want to think twice about working there. A company that is not aboveboard before you begin working certainly won't be afterward.

Let Them Save Face

As you respond to an objection, use face-saving phrases that don't attack the other person's self-image, a key factor in successful negotiations. If you make statements that can be construed as personal, you only make it harder for yourself. When someone makes a proposal that you think is ridiculous, it would be foolish on your part to answer "That's a stupid thing to say" or "You must be crazy." A more productive way to reply is, "I don't feel that is a workable alternative for me now" or "I don't think I can go along with that at this time." As Saltonstall suggests, "Always figure out a way to substitute less volatile words so that the person can hear what you have to say, appreciate what you have to say, respond positively to what you have to say and save face at the same time. If you don't leave room for the other person to save face, you put yourself at a disadvantage."

You can allow the employer to save face, especially if you are in a position to annihilate his/her argument, by attributing what you say to a third party. Your reply can now be interpreted not as a direct assault by you on him or her, but rather as a neutral third party invalidating the objection. For example, instead of saying to the employer "What you are saying is counter to everything I've seen predicted about the industry," it would be better to say, "I don't know whether you are familiar with a recent study conducted by Sticky Enterprises, Inc., but those findings suggest the trend you speak of is changing...."

The Concept of Choice

Probably the most awesome face-saving predicament to assess is the announcement by the employer early in the negotiations that his/her price is final—take it or leave it. If your experience is anything like mine, your emotions begin to take over. And of course, that's the worst thing that can happen in a negotiation. (Well, one of the worst.) With bad news such as this, we get a sinking feeling that begins to take on a life of its own. Suddenly with our aspirations chopped, we think "it's over, I've lost" and tears may spring to our eyes. We lose sight of our goals and purpose in negotiating, feel our self-worth plummet, decide we must be lucky to get any job, and give in to the employer's price.

Negative emotions snowball like this because so few of us realize that we have a choice to make when we hear something upsetting. We actually choose to react in a negative, nonproductive way by feeding one bad thought with another. The realization that one has choices is probably the most fundamental lesson a person can ever learn, not only in negotiations but in every phase of life. In its extreme, the concept of choice marks the difference between happiness and despair at both personal and professional levels. When something bad is said to us or happens to us, it is our decision to determine our behavior toward it. We can give in to our initial negative feelings and behave in a myriad of self-defeating ways: pity ourselves, lament our bad luck, blame the other person for our misfortunes. However, those who are successful and happy have learned to choose a behavior that produces better results. Harris says, "If a person changes his behavior, then the feelings are soon to follow along. In other words, the more effective you are, the better you feel about yourself. You really don't have to work first on the feelings."

So when the employer takes a position that works to your disadvantage, such as "take it or leave it," you know you have a choice to make. "How should I react to what is being said in a way that will produce the best results for me?" Focus your thoughts on what is the most appropriate means available to get around this ultimatum. You are contemplating your next move in an analytical, detached, positive manner rather than allowing runaway negative emotions to take over. Many of us react negatively because we don't have the awareness and skills to do otherwise.

Handling Ultimatums and Calling Bluffs

The constructive way to handle difficult stances in a negotiation is to remember that giving ultimatums is a tactic that frequently works in the employer's favor, and this may be why he/she is using it. It is a ploy at the employer's disposal to cut your expectations and consequently retain your services at a lower cost. Therefore, the position must be tested. You might decide to continue talking as if you didn't hear what was said. If you can offer further proof why you are worth your asking price, the employer may back off the take it or leave it position. After all, his or her face is saved. You didn't even hear that "take it or leave it"!

You might try to gently show why the employer's logic for choosing the take it or leave it figure does not apply to you. For example, "I think you will agree with me that my experience as a claims adjuster three years ago already broadens the base of the job beyond its current description." Then offer additional evidence of your potential value to him/her. Or a third technique would be to suggest that you would accept a lower figure if your salary is raised to your expectations in three months after you have had time to demonstrate your ability. By reacting positively instead of negatively to a discouraging ultimatum, you will get positive negotiating results. The only way emotion can possibly be beneficial in a negotiation is if you are using it for effect and you're not actually being controlled by it. For instance, if the employer should cast aspersions on your credentials, you might want to show mild to moderate indignation. The employer may use overkill in slighting your accomplishments as a tactic to cut your aspirations, but remember, you are not there to put up with insults. Calculating how much indignation to show is one of your own negotiating tactics.

If you should begin to feel your emotions getting a little out of control, try some self talk. Say to yourself, "I can cope with this person. It is frustrating but I can handle this situation." Or, "I'm here to get what's coming to me and I am not going to be stopped this easily." Apply relaxation techniques if you know any. There are many excellent books on the subject; read up on it. This route is far more effective than saying to yourself, "I can't handle this." Or, "He is hurting my feelings and I am going to cry." Or, "I can't cope with this." All you do with emotional negativism is fulfill your own prophecy.

Be Slow to Make Concessions

Those who don't come out well in negotiations are usually those who make the first concession, those who offer the first compromise or give in on the first point. Hold onto your opening position as long as you can. Have a negotiating goal and keep it at the forefront of your thoughts throughout the negotiation. If you lose sight of your main objective and why you're there, you will have poor results. This happens more than anybody would care to admit. Remember, people put more value on things that are harder to come by. If we make the other person work to get our price down a moderate amount, it is a more satisfying victory for him or her.

When a "No" Is Required

As I wrote this section, the widely publicized ABSCAM story broke nationally. This case has a negotiating parallel—knowing when to say "No" and having the courage to say it. ABSCAM is the case, you'll recall, where FBI agents acted as delegates of Arab sheiks to set the atmosphere for elected officials to take bribes in exchange for legislative favors. They were testing to see which politicians were honest and which were not. Believe it or not, such testing goes on in the job market too, sometimes subconsciously, and you've probably been tested by a potential employer.

Certainly on a less flamboyant scale than the FBI, employers want to know about the character of prospective employees. Some of their tactics are subtle, some not so subtle, and some would actually hold the employer's character open to question. Basically, and for good reason, they want to know if you are honest and trustworthy. For the more high-powered positions, they may want to know how much pressure you can take before you fold or whether you are predisposed to passing the buck. As an example of testing, a sales manager could tell you about a marginal practice some salespersons are using to increase their incomes. Without any indication of whether he approves or disapproves, he looks to you for a reaction. For a number of women who aren't prone to assertive behavior, the thought of giving an answer that conflicts with the employer's opinion represents an indescribable dilemma even when they fundamentally oppose the matter in question.

The typical reaction to the prospect of giving a disapproving answer is you won't get what you want, you'll lose out, or the employer won't like you. It is not easy to look a potential employer in the eye, express what may be the opposite viewpoint, and then stand by it if you are in conflict. A very real need in all of us is to be liked, but in some the need to be liked is stronger than the need to reject something that is out of character. Their tendency is to comply or fuzz up the issue quickly and change the subject, never allowing a candid discussion of honest differences. If you are one of those, you will never be a good negotiator until you change. To be successful at the bargaining table requires you to be able to say "No" when the occasion warrants.

Perhaps we tend to think about all the bad things that could possibly happen as a result of disagreeing, instead of some good that might come from it. And good can come from being selectively and respectfully contrary. That was demonstrated in the ABSCAM case by Senator Larry Pressler. While several congressmen suffered deep public humiliation because they apparently didn't know how to say an unmistakable "No," Pressler received wide and positive acclaim because he did. Not knowing his character was being tested at the time, Pressler met with FBI agents posing as businessmen in the hope of getting badly needed funds to keep his presidential campaign alive. When they tied the funds to legislative favors, the senator told them that was illegal. He said "No." As he left that meeting, odds are he was not thinking what a noble person I am to have turned down an opportunity to take a bribe. Realistically, he was probably experiencing a letdown because there would be no big contribution to his campaign. However, when his refusal was later made public by an FBI leak, the South Dakotan became an overnight national hero. Although it genuinely seems to puzzle him why anybody would be recognized for doing what they're suppose to do, it shouldn't. Right next to an inflation beater, what America loves best is an honest person, and Pressler is the only man in America who has been officially certified honest on videotape!

This story is a dramatic example of what can happen when someone has the courage to say what has to be said. But less spectacular versions of this are played out every day in the employment market. Far from alienating an employer, it may have the opposite effect. Conflict is inherent in negotiations. Successful negotiations resolve those conflicts to everyone's satisfaction. With a little patience, a good deal can usually be worked out for both parties without full capitulation on your part.

Closing the Sale

The length of time people negotiate is as varied as the people who negotiate. Choosing the right moment to close it out depends on when you think the employer is most disposed to say "yes." Only you can make that determination. However, successful people in sales will tell you that the best time to wrap up a negotiation, or "close the sale," as they say, is immediately after you have wiped out an objection to your price. The stronger the objection and the more effectively you have disposed of it, the more likely will the employer be to meet your price. After all, you have just countered his/her reason for not wanting to "buy," so why shouldn't he or she "buy"? Suggest then that you and the employer agree to your request. Say straight out, "Let's go ahead and agree on this." If he/she agrees, congratulations!

If the employer hedges, continue your presentation from where it was interrupted by the objection. You might also ask if he/she has any other concerns you might address. Remember that an objection is a record of why the employer does not want to meet your price. Consequently, when you overcome an objection, the employer is in a weaker position to resist your demands. Take advantage of this while it lasts. Suggest action by the employer. Many in sales have found this method so effective in successfully closing negotiations that they ask for objections if the other party doesn't raise them on his/her own. Say, "Do you have any questions or need further information on this?" By overcoming objections you demonstrate why your services are worth more than the money the employer will exchange for them. Once you do that, you're in business.

The assumption technique is another way to close out a negotiation in your favor. St. Louis sales executive Robert Finley says this method has worked best for him through the years. He says he doesn't like to say, "Do you think we can work something out?" Instead, he says, you should assume from the start that you are going to get what you want. Approach the closing of the negotiation with a positive attitude and actually act as though you and the employer already agree on the price in question. Summarize the main arguments for your amount and ask that it be granted. If the employer hesitates, zero in on one objection as if it were the only thing blocking your mutual agreement. Overcome the objection and then ask again for what you want. Depending on how you've sized up the other person, you might find it advantageous here to imply the negative results that may come should an agreement not be reached. The best negative argument to use in today's economic climate is double-digit inflation. Some people are motivated by a need to avoid something bad as opposed to seeking positive rewards. Indicate to him/her that any delay in starting on what has to be done right away will only increase costs. Next, reassure the employer of his/her wise move by saying "Yes, I accept." If the employer still seems hesitant, make a concession and wait quietly for an answer.

Another tip to remember: break down figure differences. If you are negotiating for $25,000 and your employer wants to pay you $22,000, don't say we're only $3,000 apart. Break it down to a weekly figure. This will naturally sound much better from the employer's viewpoint. Do some quick math in your head. Say, "Our differences are slight. We're only a little more than $50 a week apart. Let's go ahead with this."

Delay a Final Decision

Once you've bargained for the highest dollar possible for the position in question, does your agreement with the employer on a starting salary for the job commit you to the job? No, it does not. The employer has offered you a job and you both have agreed on what your salary would be should you accept the job. Nothing more. At this point, you are advised to say, "I am certainly pleased with your offer and expression of confidence in me, but I would like a couple of days to think over what we have discussed here. Perhaps we could get together again Thursday afternoon." Do this, if possible, even if you have gotten the most terrific offer you could imagine. Why? The extra time will allow you to think over whether anything was omitted in the discussion which you want covered before a final agreement is made.

Another reason for delaying a decision is that your chance of getting a more appealing package of "extra" benefits is better when you don't take on the whole ball of wax in one meeting. Confirm an appointment for another meeting. At this meeting inquire about fringe benefits and perquisites, or "perks," that would make up your total compensation package. Gently and with judgment let your preferences be known about office requirements, vacation schedules, and frequency of performance review with your first review coming after three or six months instead of the usual year. Ask about cars, credit cards, expense accounts, or whatever else might apply to you (See Chapter 6, Negotiating Extras.) Of course, if you are interviewing from out of town, you'll have to negotiate extra benefits and salary at the same meeting in all likelihood, but you can request time to think over your decision. It can be relayed in a long-distance phone call.

There are two things to keep in mind here if you feel hesitant about drawing out the process once the employer has made an offer: you get more by negotiating in pieces rather than all at once, and services are more valuable before they are delivered than after. You won't jeopardize your chance at the job by putting off your decision for a couple of days. The employer has decided that he/she wants you. A decision like that is not easily reversed. Remember, also, you've probably done quite a bit of waiting for him/her in the past few weeks or even months. If the employer should give you a specific time that he/she wants an answer, don't take the deadline too lightly. The employer may mean exactly what is said. A friend of mine missed a deadline by a day and found herself missing a job.

Perhaps the most significant reason for delaying your decision on the employer's offer is that you may want to use your negotiating results to generate an even higher offer with your current employer or with another company. A New York business executive told how this worked for her. She said she waited for an opportunity at the right time to discuss the matter with her employer and inquired in a low-key, nonthreatening manner why her work was worth 20 percent more to the other employer than to him. She said, "He just shook his head and walked out, but the next thing I knew I had been bounced up substantially. He got the message." It is a highly compelling force when somebody else wants to hire you. If you have other strong and interesting leads, by all means call them and tell them about your offer and that you are nearing a decision on it. You may kick off some surprising developments. The only time perhaps you should not delay a decision on terms of employment is if it is one of those once-in-a-lifetime offers and you recognize it as such. Maybe the employer was acting impulsively on that day.

On the other hand, it is not uncommon for the employer to say he/she wants time to think over your requests before reaching a final agreement on salary. You may have convinced him/her that you are worth more than the employer originally intended to pay for the job. He/she may have to discuss your demands with others in the company. When that happens, make a firm agreement on a time when a decision will be forthcoming. If the employer says, "I'll have to think about this" and you nod in compliance and walk away, you leave yourself open to "twist slowly in the wind." Instead, say, "How much time do you need?" Or "Let's get together next Monday." Or, "when is a convenient time for us to get together again?"

Avoid Phone Negotiations

The employer will probably call you in a couple of days on the phone to say she/he either agrees or doesn't agree to your request. Don't pursue the negotiations on the phone. Suggest a time for a meeting. Usually the employer has caught you by surprise when he/she calls and you may not be at your best. This advice holds also when an employer calls you to offer a job and encourages you to agree to a figure then and there over the phone. A quick negotiation under these circumstances tends to work against you. It's best whenever possible to negotiate face to face. On the phone you can't see how the person is reacting to what you are saying and it is easier for the employer to say "No" when he/she doesn't have to look at you. When you have no choice but to negotiate on the phone, tell the employer you will call him/her back after you've had a chance to think over the proposal.

Because of the uniqueness of negotiations—no two are ever alike—there may be times when you feel you are at the banquet of life with no fork. When uncharted courses arise, it's better to use your common sense than to freeze, fearing to move one way or the other. Pragmatically, in the give and take of negotiating, you are going to win a few and lose a few, but at least you won't be losing them all.

FIVE

Skillful Answers to Difficult Questions and Other Tactics

Employers Are Not Negotiating Experts

We can only begin to successfully negotiate when we realize that it's not enough to be good at our jobs. We have to know how to effectively make demands in exchange for energetic and productive performances in the work force. No longer can we settle on being grateful for getting a chance at better jobs. It is time to ask for the rewards that go with responsibility. It is time to negotiate.

When you negotiate a job offer, you have good reason to be self-confident. Dr. Ralph Minker, a Washington-based career consultant, says you are like a "big fat trout in the middle of a mountain stream. They want you." By now, you've probably met several times with the employer and perhaps others in the organization. They have sunk time on you. They've discussed you among themselves. You quite likely have won out over a number of other candidates. At least one of the persons on the management team may be your champion and it may or may not be the person with whom you are negotiating. Perhaps your potential employer's boss said "get her." The one thing the person who is doing the actual hiring will not want to do is come back to his/her manager and say "she got away." Being in this situation does not mean you can begin to give ultimatums, but it does mean you should continue with the same style that got you this far.

Keep in mind that most managers are not experts in hiring people. The interviewing and negotiating process is an interruption to what they ordinarily do and to what they probably prefer to do. Sometimes employers are lax about their hiring practices or just haven't thought enough about them. All they may want to do is just get the hiring over with in the most expedient manner. Some don't care whether it is the most efficient way or not. What you can do is help them help you. You can help them manage intelligently by successfully demonstrating your skills so that they give you the opportunity to use your abilities on behalf of their organization in exchange for fair compensation. If the right sort of interviewing has taken place, there should be no questions at this point about the content or the context of the job. Now it is a matter of a financial package.

Minker advises you to take notes in a negotiation. He says, and quite accurately, that most people wouldn't think of approaching something of real importance without taking notes. Experience shows that not many of us can boast of total recall and, further, notetaking shows your seriousness, your attention to detail, and your thoroughness. By taking notes, you flatter the individual by indicating that he or she has something to say worth writing down. You show some of the characteristics of the professional that person wishes to employ.

What Were You Earning on Your Last Job?

At some juncture in the negotiation, the employer is likely to ask your earnings on your current or past job. Since employers tend to base offers on previous salaries, you might, if your history is typical, put yourself at a negotiating disadvantage when you reveal this figure. There are two schools of thought on how you should answer the previous salary question. Choose the approach you are most comfortable with.

The first approach is to answer the question bluntly and directly. If you are earning $275 a week, you would say you are earning $275 a week. Personnel professionals, in particular, have advised me that any effort to fuzz up your answer may cast doubt on the credibility of your performance record, not to mention your candor. They advise that you should give the correct figure and (without saying, "but I was underpaid") explain in firm terms that the figure is not representative of your worth. You might say you are prepared to assume more responsibility, which you expect will lead to higher earnings. You might point out that women in your line of work are often paid less than men and that you are looking for employment where you feel the pay structure is fair.

The second approach to the past salary question is the one I prefer. You're not being untruthful, but you are being less direct. As it has been said, the art of answering questions lies in knowing what to say and what not to say. It does not lie in being right or wrong. There is a better way to answer the question of previous earnings than to say the truth. Instead of, "On my past job, I was earning $227.50 after taxes," give yourself your upcoming raise. Say "By the end of the year, I will be earning $15,000." If you feel cornered, you don't have to state a specific figure. Say "I'm earning in the midteens." That could be anything from $14,000 to $17,000. Or you might say, "When I get my expected promotion, my financial package will be in the neighborhood of $18,000." (Fringe benefits often reach 25 to 30 percent over and beyond a base salary.)

Then add, "But I am sure we both know that whatever salary I should receive from your company will be in line with the level of responsibility I will be entrusted with rather than what I have been doing on my other job." You are showing a firmness and a clarity about yourself and you're not being argumentative. By stressing the relationship between level of salary and level of responsibility, you are actually being very logical and reasonable.

Low Earnings Trap

The question of past salary being asked is disturbing to me because it catches women in a low earnings trap, almost impossible to escape. Employers will use that figure to establish your worth regardless of what your accomplishments have been. I agree with Minker, who says management's question about previous earnings is based on ineptness. (Although I do concede that some managers recognize the question for what it is—a convenient way, in many cases, to keep their costs down.) After all, that was a different job, different organization, different budget structure, and perhaps a different point as far as the cost-of-living is concerned. You may be negotiating now with a company that may, because of the nature of this particular business, put more value on someone with your skills. The employer should expect to pay you for the value you represent to him/her, not the value you've been to someone else. Minker gives this illustration. "If I want somebody to play first base for the Baltimore Orioles and we want to win the pennant, I will pay what is necessary to get the talent to play first base. I don't care what the person has been making. I want some productivity at first base." Remember to press to be paid at the level appropriate for the responsibility you anticipate performing. You should be paid for what you are going to do in your new company rather than on the basis of what you were doing for another company.

What if you've been doing volunteer work and have no prior earnings? You really are at an acute disadvantage in a discussion of salary. And since you've learned valuable skills rendering volunteer services, being penalized for having low or no earnings is not fair. Say something to the effect, "Had I been earning at the level of my abilities, I would have been making (*name a figure*)." If you've been at home with children, have done no volunteer work, and have no prior earnings, you can try naming a figure you think is fair and ask to be given a trial period at that level during which you will demonstrate successfully why you're worth that salary. It is far more equitable to make a case for what all your experience is actually worth based on your abilities. Otherwise, your earnings are doomed to reflect your unsatisfying history of low or no earnings, a history that will perpetuate itself.

Verifying Prior Earnings

You may wonder whether employers verify salary information. If the figure sounds totally unrealistic, they should check and probably will. However, new privacy laws are making it more difficult for employers to secure information on employees. It is the policy of some companies to say nothing about the employee except to verify employment, but it seems most companies go a little further. The most common procedure used by employers is for the potential employer to call a former employer and say that an employee has indicated that he or she earned at a level of such and such. Then they ask for verification—"Is that true?" The former employer can respond with a simple yes or no answer. Therefore, make sure the justification for the figure you give to the employer is clearly defined as illustrated in the examples we've just discussed.

Regardless of how you choose to answer the question of prior earnings, write "open" or "negotiable" in the application blank on salary requirements. Or write, "I am ready to discuss salary in terms relative to the responsibility I am being asked to assume."

"We Like You, But..."

In addition to the past salary question, there are other questions or statements you can expect to field during a negotiation, especially if you are making high demands. For example, the employer may say, "We like you but we do have other strong candidates if we can't resolve our salary differences." Again, you might use the tactic of continuing to talk as if you didn't hear what was said. Offer further proof of why you're worth your asking price.

If you believe the employer may be close to breaking off the negotiations, however, you might suggest that you would like a day or two to think about the discussions and then confirm another appointment. A little breathing space may allow the next meeting to be conducted on a more harmonious note. And the extra time can be used for you to decide whether you want to risk forgoing the offer or to determine the nature of your next concession. Regardless of what you decide to do, the point is—if you are not prepared to go further in a negotiation at that moment, you generally don't have to.

Others Aren't Making That Much

If the employer says, "How much more did you have in mind?" (assuming the employer named a low figure first), give a definite figure. Say, for example, "We could wrap it up at $21,000" or whatever is an appropriate figure for your negotiating situation. Or state, "I had expected to make $21,000 when I changed jobs." The employer may retort that others on the staff with more experience aren't earning the salary you want. That's really the employer's problem and doesn't warrant a reply on your part. I can't caution you too much to keep in mind who controls what. Don't take the employer's management responsibilities upon yourself.

In this case, however, you might opt to acknowledge that there will always be someone with more experience, but the employer has indicated—and you agree—that the emphasis should be placed on high performance and demonstrated ability to successfully dissolve obstacles in the path of a job well-done. Conclude by saying, "If my record of achievement can help you meet your objectives, won't that be worth my fair market value?"

Your Price Won't Fit Our Budget

If the employer says "I'm sorry, but your asking price won't fit into our budget," you might reply, "I know that in many businesses today it is a standard practice to give up to three thousand dollars in extra salary after six months. What about that in terms of our agreement?" You can't force it, but you can help the employer help you solve the problem. You can give him or her an alternative to work with. You are making it easy for the employer to accommodate you.

A performance review after an orientation period is a good idea because it is a way to measure whether the new employee is on the right track. It is also recognition by the employer that the employee is producing what was hoped for. In fact, because the employer may discover that the employee is doing better than expected, the three- to six-month performance review makes a good rationale for a salary increase.

Increases: Cost-of-Living versus Merit

Another important aspect of salary negotiating is to inquire about increment policies. There are two. One is an increase in earnings based on merit, or how well you have performed over a given period of time. The second is cost-of-living, which is tied to the country's inflationary economy. The issue of increment policies is significant. If you can negotiate for both cost-of-living and merit increases, you will obviously be better off than those who get only one or the other. Say, "We have been talking about basic salary, but I assume that this organization would have an annual adjustment aside from my merit increase. Is that so?"

Another way of expressing the distinction between a cost-of-living raise and a merit increase is to discuss your professional future. You might say, "While the starting salary is important to me, I am also concerned about my future. When I am evaluated, will it be on my demonstrated worth to the company or will it be solely a mechanical upgrading?" The only answer, of course, is that you will be evaluated on your demonstrated worth. It would be difficult for an employer to say otherwise. Since cost-of-living adjustments are fairly common these days, you might be able to secure a promise of a merit raise for yourself over and beyond the cost-of-living increment by phrasing the inquiry this way.

Flexibility

It is wise to stay flexible in salary negotiations. Using a sports vernacular to illustrate this point, Minker says, "In football, if you are a back, you are taught to run certain patterns... three steps this way, three that way ... but the really great runners are those who run for daylight. They know how to run patterns but they also know how to improvise, how to be flexible. They don't run into a three-hundred pounder because the coach told them to run three steps in that direction!"

As a negotiator, you will have to determine what is most likely to work for you in each instance. Each game, like each negotiation, is different. This book provides you with ideas and suggestions, but only you know what is truly appropriate for you.

Precedents

Employers are especially concerned that their conceding to demands not set a bad precedent. Will their decision with one employee bind them with all others? If you sense the employer is resisting your request for this reason, change the time or money designations of your demand. Stick with the high amount but suggest that part of it be paid at the end of a three- or six-month period, after you have sufficiently demonstrated your value to the company.

Faced with some other strong refusal for the salary you are negotiating, you might ask to have your job description broadened at the outset so the salary would be commensurate with your wider duties. Thus when an employer implies that your asking price won't fit into the budget, be flexible—adopt a flexible posture openly with the employer. Alter the conditions of your demands.

Think on Your Feet

I discussed thinking on your feet with a woman who heads a data-processing firm in Washington. We agreed that swift thinking on your feet is required to counter many of the arguments hurled at you in a negotiation. She recalled being stumped for quick comebacks to remarks made to her. And she believes, as I do, that because women are naive negotiators, we need more "thinking time." Job interviews are helpful in this respect. They provide good practice in learning how to control and direct the dialogue for your benefit, how to present yourself, and how to deal with different types of personalities.

Don't panic if, even after rehearsing, you are asked a question you just don't have the slightest idea of how to answer. Simply say, "That question requires thought and I will see that you get the quality of response you are seeking at our next meeting." You might also say, "I'll put the information in a letter to you tomorrow," or "I don't know, but I'll try to find out for you." Don't be surprised if you pick up points by making such an acknowledgment.

A ranking company officer asked the identical question to four candidates for the same high-paying position. Three of the candidates answered the question without hesitation, rapidly resolving the problem addressed in the question. The fourth candidate listened, reflected for a moment, and then announced that the question was too complicated to answer without considerable thought. This candidate got the job. Why? It seems the employer had spent a great deal of time finding the answer and appreciated recognition of the problem's difficulty. When the other candidates rolled off quick solutions, he was nonplussed. Besides, their answers made him feel that they might come to regard him as slow-witted should they learn how long it took him to find an answer to a question they regarded as easy!

SIX

Negotiating Extras

Fringe Benefits

"Men are not born knowing about pension plans," said a man to one woman I interviewed. "Go out and find the answers like everybody else." This perspective might help if you're feeling apprehensive learning about fringe benefits. These extra rewards, usually of a non-monetary nature, nevertheless represent real cash value. While salary makes up the lion's share of the total compensation package, national figures suggest that fringe benefits can add another 30 percent to your earnings. As management consultant Sandra O'Connell says, "In certain salary ranges where there are profit sharing, stock options and bonuses, I know people who double their salary. And women aren't paying close enough attention to the overall compensation package."

In a negotiation, the time to pay attention to fringe benefits is after you have negotiated for the highest possible salary. Then turn your negotiating skills toward securing the best package of benefits.

Benefits: Fixed and Flexible

Basically, there are two kinds of fringe benefits. First of all, there are those that are fixed and apply to all employees equally. The group health and pension or retirement plans of most companies are set. The president of a company often has the same coverage benefits as a secretary. However, other fringe benefits are more flexible and are scaled by job category or job level. These perquisites or "perks" may include such tangibles as:

- a larger office with better furniture
- first-class travel
- limousine service to the airport
- free medical examinations
- extra insurance coverage
- credit cards
- expense accounts
- relocation expenses
- low-interest loans
- flexible hours
- company cars for business and sometimes for personal use also
- stock options whereby employees can purchase company stock at a generally reduced market rate
- free or inexpensive financial and legal counseling such as help in preparing tax forms and writing wills
- deferred compensation plans that allow the company to pay you part of your earnings at a future date for tax benefits
- club memberships and dues for professional associations
- extra vacation time
- tuition refund plans to reimburse employees for job-related studies
- thrift or savings plans where the employer matches a portion of the employee's savings

Negotiating for "Perks"

Middle management is the level where you can usually expect to begin acquiring valuable perks, depending on the industry and your position in it. Undoubtedly, it would serve you well to consult your peers before you negotiate to find out what kind of perks they have and whether they know about the perks connected with the job you are considering. But even if you're not in middle management and you're going into a job at the professional level, you should be informed enough to ask about the company's compensation program

beyond salary and at what point one is eligible for the various benefits. Say, "What kind of program do you have in additional benefits
for management?" Then inquire, "At what point do I become eligible for them?"

You can't be reticent about getting information. By putting off
discussion of "extras" until this late in the process, you've sufficiently demonstrated to the employer that you understand priorities. If
the employer says the company doesn't offer a program of perquisites, at least you are aware of some of the extra benefits for which
you might negotiate on your own.

For those just entering the job market, one of the better benefits
available will probably be a tuition refund plan. Companies take
pride in these educational assistance programs and tend to notice an
employee's serious effort at self-improvement. Another perk that
may be open to those on the lower rungs of the business ladder is a
thrift or savings plan.

How to Avoid Missing Out on Perks

There are scores of tales about how women have missed out on
perks. Sometimes it is not enough to ask the employer about these
benefits before you begin a job. You have to keep your eyes and
ears open after you are working at your new position. A female vice
president of an international corporation relayed the following story
to me. She said when she was promoted to vice president, she had
inquired of the vice president in charge of personnel about the perks
she might receive only to be told, "Perks, what perks? We don't have
perks." She persisted. "There must be four weeks of vacation and a
limousine to go to the airport." He said, "Oh sure, you can have
that." Sometime later she was driving with a colleague in her modest
little Pinto when he asked where was her company car. She knew
nothing about a company car, but she found that all the other vice
presidents in her division had cars as part of their compensation
package. She then went back to the vice president of personnel and
said, "I have learned that all vice presidents have company cars. I
don't know if you are trying to tell me something—that I am a
second-class vice president—but I would appreciate it if you would

look into this and let me know." When no one acted on her request, she then mentioned it to her boss. She kept the pressure on until she finally got the car. But even then she was slighted. The company provides cars in three price ranges according to job level. Although she was eligible for a car in the second range, she was authorized to get one at the cheapest level. When you don't negotiate and persevere, your employer will give you as little as possible. You can't sit around waiting for perks to be offered to you. They can be hard to get even when you do negotiate and persevere.

An executive recruiter I interviewed says he thinks preoccupation with fringe benefits in a negotiation is only for the insecure and the time-servers. I don't believe that and I do believe your first priority should be to negotiate for the highest dollar you can get. But you should then turn your attention toward acquiring the best package of benefits. Using your judgment, let your preferences be known for whatever extras are important to you. Perhaps you like to take your vacation at Christmas or to do your research away from the main office. Career consultant Hal Shook of Life Management Services, Inc. concurs, "When you go as far as you can with the cash in negotiating, then start on the fringe benefits. Maybe you can request a more frequent salary review, or stock options or a car. We've had people go in and ask for an office overlooking the river!"

Contracts and Written Agreements

"When and only when you're sure he wants you, and he has made a firm job offer, negotiate. And when (and if) it is resolved to your satisfaction, get it in writing, please. The road to hell is paved with verbal promises made in the heat of hiring that were never fulfilled." Those are the wise words of Richard Nelson Bolles in his book *What Color Is Your Parachute?* *

When you've concluded a negotiation where mutually agreeable terms have been reached, I would advise you to cover the terms in a letter to the employer as soon as possible. Say something like for the sake of communications it is your understanding that you will be do-

*Ten Speed Press, Berkeley, Calif., 1976. Reprinted with permission.

ing such and such job. Then describe the duties and responsibilities you will be expected to perform and mention when your performance review is to take place. Indicate how your performance is to be measured and the criteria for success, along with your compensation. Don't leave out any extras you've negotiated. Bill O'Keefe, vice president of the American Petroleum Institute, says, "As a general rule there would be nothing wrong with making sure that there is complete understanding between the prospective employee and the employer. One way to do that is to lay out your understanding of what you are going to be expected to do. How much detail you go into depends on the specific job." Many letters of agreement can be written on a page or two.

Letter of Agreement

A letter of agreement has been likened to an apartment house lease: it can be broken. Because people can quit or be fired, the bet can be off. But if you stay on the job, your letter is a record, in black and white, of what the employer expects of you and what you expect from the employer. A letter of agreement is a document that establishes terms and conditions of your work. It is something that you can refer to six, nine, or twelve months from the time you go on the payroll to determine whether the conditions of employment are being met.

Occasionally an employee will not want to do anything beyond what the letter of agreement or the job description calls for. And that disturbs some employers, who may not have anticipated certain duties at the time the employee was hired. The employee who really moves ahead is eager to take on additional responsibilities. He or she knows that expanding the base of the job is the surest way to build a case for a raise or a promotion. Your written agreement says you were hired for specific tasks and now you are doing those tasks plus others equally important. It is the best justification for higher earnings.

Initiate the Agreement

Once a job offer has been extended and the compensation negotiated, it is not uncommon for an employer to confirm the offer in writing. The employee is told in the letter that he or she will be receiving a certain salary, will be entitled to certain benefits, and, generally, when performance will be reviewed. Although some companies do make well-defined job descriptions available to the employee, the measurements of success on the job are rarely addressed. That's why I urge you to write your letter as soon after the negotiation as you can—before you receive the employer's letter. It is to your advantage to initiate the written agreement. As author Chester Karrass* says, "It is simply one method of getting the area of agreement laid out in one's own way rather than leaving it to the other person." To reemphasize, say at the beginning of the letter that you are writing to ensure mutual understanding in connection with your employment and conclude by saying that you would appreciate correction of any inaccuracies in what you have said.

Job Contracts

If you are going into a newly created job or one in which there has been turmoil and turnover, you might want to be even more formal and discuss the possibility of an employment contract with the employer. These legally binding contracts tend to be limited in some organizations to key executives. For example, one executive told me he requested an employment contract when he was asked to help turn around a money-losing firm that was family owned and operated. He also required that specific details be spelled out on the company's prerogatives—in other words, exactly what was to be accomplished and what the measure for judging performance would be. And it was to be agreed that if he were fired for whatever reason, he would walk away with a sizable cash payoff.

If you are in a strong negotiating position where you feel an employment contract is appropriate, you will probably want to retain an attorney to look over the terms of agreement before you sign anything. Don't bring one directly into the negotiations as this will not

* *Give and Take*, Copyright © 1974 by Chester L. Karrass. Reprinted by permission of Harper & Row Publishers, Inc.

show your own abilities in the best light. As executive recruiter Dick Irish says, "The worst possible thing that could happen would be to show up at a final negotiation with your next employer and have your attorney in tow. Maybe that would be appropriate for a tennis star, athlete, or artist. That's an entirely different relationship, because they are selling a name, a celebrity, a certain specific talent for a certain specific assignment. If you are hiring an executive for an unspecified length of time to give leadership to an organization and every leader has to take a few risks. . . . A person who is going to protect his or her interests to the extent that he or she is going to take no risk in taking a job, in my judgment, is not qualified for an important job."

Proposals

"Get off your knees," says well-known career consultant John Crystal. He describes the usual job hiring experience as this: the employee going before the employer with "hat in hand, begging for a position, powerless to negotiate." Instead of this, Crystal says you should remember that "you are a dignified human being who has unique talents and skills. Figure out what you want to do with your life. Then make your job congruent with your personal goals. Select an organization you would like to work for, research its history and functions, find out who has the power to hire you and submit a proposal." When you submit a proposal to someone in a position to hire you, the process becomes a "business conference of equals." The hiring procedure, says Crystal, is the "only aspect of our lives where we have somehow been conned into thinking we must assume the attitude of the slave before the master."

Business Conference of Equals

In an interview in U.S. *News & World Report,** Crystal was asked how important are salary negotiations. His reply: "Extremely important. How many people do you know who ever have had any training in bargaining the way union and management negotiators

*Reprinted from *U.S. News & World Report* (March 12, 1979)

do? It's simple once you know how. But most of us don't even know we're allowed to do this. Under the traditional system, we go into a job interview with fear and trembling. We feel we're there to be judged and we'll accept anything. This is particularly true to women. They're often afraid to bargain. Let's say you are thinking of hiring me for your company and plan to send me to Atlanta to represent your organization in a business situation. If I don't even try to negotiate for myself, how well do you think I'll bargain for your company in Atlanta? But if I come across to you as a polite, talented, diplomatic but skillful negotiator, your opinion of me is bound to go up. I keep stressing that people need to learn the truth about bargaining . . . the things we don't tell youngsters in high school, all the things we've carefully kept from women, come to think of it. Few of us realize that once we get above the job level where we're considered replaceable parts of a machine and move into the category where individual talent and ability to make decisions count. That's where the boss is going to listen to your proposal and say, 'here's some talent I need.' " © 1979 U.S. News and World Report, Inc.

Key to Higher Earnings

Career consultant Hal Shook agrees with Crystal on the importance of proposals. He says, "The whole key to getting a better salary is to increase your value, which you can do with a proposal. If a woman discovers she is being paid less, I would suggest that she think in terms of a proposal aimed at increasing her value. It would certainly be more effective than saying so and so is making more money than I am."

In devising a proposal you are forced to think about the other person's needs. Ask yourself what you can do to increase your value to them. The characteristics of a successful proposal include answers to several questions: What is the problem or need? What is the solution? What return can the company expect? Why me above everybody else? What is it going to cost? Shook advises you to write a proposal for every final target you are going after. Some proposals can be written on half a page and some delivered orally. When you present a proposal, don't give it all away. Give them just enough information so that they will want more. Otherwise, they might take your proposal and not you. It happens to naive people all the time.

Pay Attention to Presentation

If your proposal doesn't make sense, of course, you can't bargain, but if it does have merit, the other party is going to figure out how to get you. To ensure acceptance of your proposal, pay attention to your presentation. Public relations consultant Beverly Jackson says the slicker the proposal looks, the better it seems to be received. She says, "We have proposal covers designed and we put our bound proposals inside a proposal kit. We make a big deal out of it even when it is only a two or three page item." It is also a courtesy to give people extra copies in case they have to give one to their budget officer or executive officer. Then you know that all the copies you have given them are of good quality rather than relying on the other person's copying facility, which may or may not be of high grade.

Bravado

Kathleen Bowers, who owns her own personnel business, says "bravado" should accompany any proposal. She says, "There's a lot to be said for bravado because I think people look at people who seem to be very confident and successful and they don't know you are scared to death. I've met certain women in business and I wonder how they stay in business. There is no aura about them of being confident or successful. I doubt if they ever do succeed." But many women are getting past the handicap of "no aura."

Bowers and I both think the female entrepreneur is way out front in this regard. This special breed knows they are in business to make money and they are gaining the confidence to ask for a fair return on their services. One of these independent types was negotiating recently with a company executive, who remarked that she was "one tough woman" to deal with, never giving an inch. She replied that, given the assignment, this should be a plus. He filled in the rest, saying, "You've hit the nail on the head. That's the reason we want you so much." She uses wit and wisdom without edging over the line that offends people. Her style gets action on her proposals.

SEVEN

Building A Negotiating Base

Raise-Reducing Tactics

I knew I had been sandbagged, but not being a negotiator, I didn't know what to say or do. My employer had just said, "You are one of the most valuable people on my staff, but I can't give you the raise you deserve this year because things are so tight. The only way I can swing it is to fire someone. Do you want me to fire someone so you can have a big raise and if so, who do you want me to fire?" As I look back on it, I see how this was a bewildering ploy for a manager to use. But what is even more bewildering is that it worked, at least momentarily. "Oh, don't fire anybody because of me!" I said without hesitating. And that was exactly what he wanted to hear. He had played on my emotions and as a nonnegotiator, I had fallen for it.

I shudder to think how many women are witless victims of such raise-reducing tactics. Part of the bottom-line game plan in business is to keep us feeling grateful for our responsible positions so that we will work for lower salaries, or as in my case, so I would be content knowing that I had "saved" somebody's job. That experience brought home to me my pitiful lack of negotiating skills and it served as a springboard for a whole new set of thoughts and attitudes toward work. I began to learn how to negotiate.

I asked several women how they would have answered that question had they been in my shoes. One said, "Why not suggest that he fire himself?" Another said, "Suggest that your raise come from his salary!" I suppose not everybody can carry it off without hostility, but humor is an effective tool in some of these situations. I particularly liked the tactic offered by career advisor John J. Tarrant.* He says to paint a doomsday picture yourself. Say, "Tell me, just how bad are things around here? How much time do you think we have before the bottom falls out?" Your employer is not likely to want rumors of financial doom flying and will quite logically back off.

If I had it to do over, I would respond in one of two ways. First, acting as though the proposal wasn't serious, I would ignore it. As negotiators we must keep in mind who controls what; never assume reponsibility for issues in the manager's court. In my case I couldn't do anything about who gets fired—that was my employer's problem— but I could do something about me. Had I been a negotiator, I would have known that the company was making more money than it had the previous year. I would have been prepared to relate my duties to those profits and would have tied my request to the normal cost of doing business.

The second way I might have handled that situation would be to indicate gently but assertively that if he felt economically constrained to grant what I considered a fair and responsible request, I might not be able to put in the extra hours I worked as a matter of course. A good employer is likely to conclude that someone is going to have to be paid to take up the slack and it might as well be you. You have to be careful how you do this. You shouldn't go off in a huff and say from now on I'm just going to punch the time clock. Be subtle.

Relate Your Work to Profits

The first misconception of mine to bite the dust was that if I

*How to Negotiate a Raise by John J. Tarrant, © by Litton Educational Publishing, Inc., 1976. Reprinted by permission of Van Nostrand Reinhold Company.

worked hard, I would be justly rewarded. What naivete! Getting good at what you do and then waiting around for financial justice to be heaped on you without any effort on your part reflects massive ignorance of business and its profit-making quest. Coupled with competency has to be an awareness of business politics and even more fundamentally, how your job relates to the company's bottom line, or in other words, how much your skills are contributing to company profits. If you can't relate your job to the bottom line, how can you make an effective presentation for a raise which suggests that your worth to the company has increased? All of this is especially difficult for women because most of us don't work at jobs that can be reduced easily to the bottom line such as marketing and engineering functions. In fact, the Bureau of Labor Statistics in Washington reports that 80 percent of working women are involved in service-oriented or knowledge businesses like banking and insurance.

Defining Jobs

Defining a service job requires time and commitment from top management. In the interests of your future negotiations with a company, it is important that you discuss your job definition during the interviewing process. "It is enormously difficult for an individual to try to bring a job down to the bottom line for a performance evaluation if the management layers above have hazy goals about service-area jobs," says Edward A. Grefe, president of International Civics, Inc. in New York. "The definition process has to start at the top."

One of the best ways to determine what kind of priority a corporation places on service jobs is to look at the organizational chart to see to whom people report. If there is a direct line from your service-oriented department to the Chief Executive Officer (CEO), then goals for service jobs will probably be clearly defined and more highly valued. For example, as you look at the accompanying organizational chart of a major American corporation, you will see that the director of the service-oriented Personnel Department reports directly to the CEO or in this case, the general manager. Also, the fact that the senior officer of your department has a background in

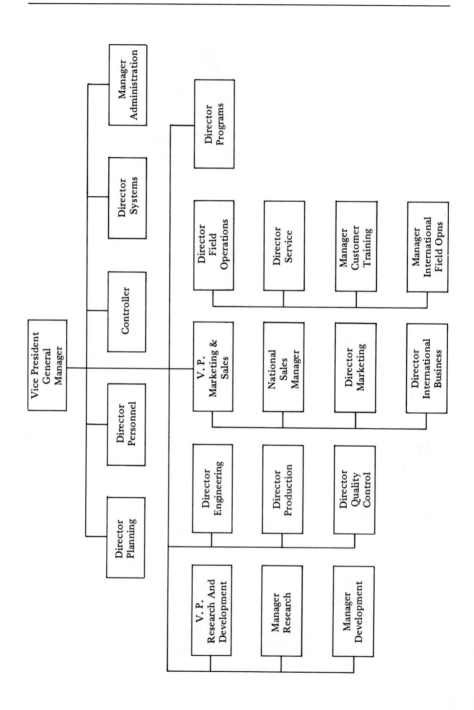

the area he or she is charged with running would be another strong indication that service jobs are considered important in terms of corporate profits. Sometimes you may discover a CEO who feels uncomfortable quantifying service jobs, choosing not to deal with this function. That explains why a CEO may take a loyal, long-time employee who may not be measuring up to full expectations in a hard area like sales and put him or her at the head of a service department like personnel, public relations, or public affairs. The decision results in having someone in charge who knows nothing about the department, leaving it up to the ill-equipped department head to define, or rather ill-define, jobs that are up to him or her to fill.

Questions to Ask

You will have to ask certain questions outright to have enough information to accurately assess the company. If you are offered a job, you will want to know if it is a brand new position. You will want to try to find out about the person for whom you will be working—how much does the boss know? You have to interview the other person. You might say, "Tell me about yourself. Have you been with the company long?" Ask for a precise definition of what is expected of you. Ask about the CEO's view of this department's goals. How long did the previous person have the job? What happened to him or her? How many people preceded that person in this position? And inquire about the growth of the company. Grefe adds, "If people have been on the job for awhile, it is probably a happy company."

Management consultant O'Connell continues along these lines when she stresses the need to get clear standards, objectives, and agreements before you undertake a job. Ask how your results will be measured. That way when you begin a job, you lay good groundwork on which to get top raises in the future. With this type of question asking, your performance will be much less prone to subjective evaluation.

The Profit Theme

My advice is to clear up anything that you can no matter where you are on the organization chart. Many people wisely define their jobs to their own advantage. Wherever there is a void of responsibility, there is an opportunity to fill it in and benefit not only your organization but yourself. The world of business is not a perfect place. Management consultant Gonnie Siegel says, "I have yet to see the CEO who isn't grateful for an employee's attempt to define his or her job if there is no definition of it anywhere else. And if there is, add to it." If you've been in your position for a while, then you are the person who knows your job best. You know what you do. You also know better ways of doing it, improvements that could be made. Siegel continues, "It is corny but true that if you find a way to increase profits, you can write your own ticket. This separates the free enterprise system from the rest of the world. Take advantage of it."

Women, in particular, because they have traditionally been givers, must get comfortable with the idea of profits. It is a theme that runs through their lives and it does not work in the business world except to exploit those who are uncomfortable with it. Profit is not a bad word. We need to understand that we aren't "greedy" by simply getting a fair return on our own efforts.

Compensation Is Always Changing

Women need better insights into the arena of compensation to strengthen negotiating skills. One of the first things you need to know, says Martin-Marietta's director of compensation, John Gordy, "is that the compensation business is constantly changing." Many companies conduct regular salary surveys and update their ranges because it is in their self-interest to keep their salaries competitive. Gordy says, "You have to know what is going on in the marketplace. For example, if engineers right out of school this year are going to start around $19,000 and if I'm looking for an engineer at $15,000, I'm not even in the ballpark. If we say we are going to hire three engineers at an average of $19,000 and we find a superstar that's going to cost us $20,500, we will pay it."

This points up an old axiom in business that if the company wants you and you are really worth it, it will find a way to pay for you. A leading corporate executive says "When push comes to shove, managers have a pot of money to fall back on." If they don't have the extra money, there are other ways to sweeten the offer. One woman I heard about bargained to do her work outside the main office in New York. She does her research from a beach house at Cape Cod. Gordy says if his company's salary survey valued a certain job at $28,500 and a prospective employee came in requesting $30,000, he or she might get it. "If he or she was an outstanding performer," says Gordy, "and I knew the company across the street would hire that person, I would give the extra $1,500." However, O'Connell maintains that many rank and file managers don't have that kind of clout in salary matters. "Managers have more constraints on them today than they ever had in the past. Most of them operate on distribution curves which drive them nuts. Last year some were on a seven percent cap which mean if they gave somebody a ten percent raise, then somebody else got four percent." But, cautions O'Connell, there are always exceptions. "I have a colleague who bought that story. She thought the seven percent was fair and all that could be done only to find out that one of her male co-workers had received a 20 percent increase in salary. And his performance rating was not as high as hers. It happened that the man was in a different division where the manager was more inclined to fight."

The Other Person's Power

This brings us to another curve in the negotiating road. You need to know about the power of the person with whom you are negotiating. Does he or she make the decisions? Or are these powers coming from someone else? If you don't know, inquire diplomatically. It is definitely easier to negotiate with a person who does call the shots. A person with limited negotiating authority has to consult with a higher-up before any firm agreement can be reached. Some companies like all their managers to negotiate from a position of "limited authority." It is a good negotiating tactic from their side but not from yours. These managers can always claim that it is not they but some faceless committee or other person rejecting your requests. If you recognize this, it will save you a lot of frustration and perhaps encourage you to persevere with a little more fortitude. Keep feeding good arguments for your requests that the manager can pass along to the real decision maker.

Job Classifications

You'll want to know about salary ranges, how the ranges are determined, and what it takes to get into another range. Generally, your job classification is synonymous with your job title. The main thing a company wants to do in classifying people is to maintain consistency. All directors should be performing the functions of a director as defined by the company. Certain titles—chiefs, managers, vice presidents— are used specifically for supervisory types of jobs, while other titles—specialist, representative, accountant, or buyer—signify nonsupervisory jobs.

When it comes to classifying and evaluating jobs to determine what various functions are worth on the job market, there are probably eight or ten ways it is done. Many companies have very formal evaluation systems, whereas others are more subjective in their evaluations. This whole question of job evaluations—how jobs are evaluated—promises to be a growing issue during the 1980s. We are not as likely to be hearing "equal pay for equal work" as we are "equal pay for work of comparable value."

One evaluation system that is frequently used is based on points. Certain aspects of a job are assigned a predetermined number of points after the level of skills required to execute the duties is analyzed. When all the points connected with any given job are added up, naturally, the higher numbers represent the better paying jobs. Then there is the factor comparison system where a company takes a portion of a job and compares it to another. A third system that seems to be more subjective but actually may be just as accurate in the long run requires a committee to rank the jobs in a company from top to bottom.

Job Openings

Before you can move from one classification to a higher one, there

must be an opening. That occurs when somebody leaves or is promoted or when the workforce is expanded. The better managed
companies have policies to make their employees aware of openings
and how to go about applying for them. If you are going into a new
job or if you've been on the job for a while and don't know how to
apply for a higher position, ask your prospective employer or inquire
at the personnel office. It seems the usual procedure is to post openings on bulletin boards with instructions on how to apply for them if
you feel you are qualified. The real go-getters are ahead of the bulletin board. In the negotiating process, however, you should inquire
about salary ranges, how they are arrived at, and how you can move
into a higher one. Showing some understanding of salary in a negotiation is important in helping you to get the best financial results,
not just immediately but over the long haul.

The Big Raise

How well you negotiate depends on how badly you need or want
the job. That's what one manager told me and I have no doubt, with
human nature being what it is, he is correct. But it doesn't have to
be that way. If we really want something, our conditions tend to be
far more malleable than they would be if our interest was only luke-
warm. Thus we hear stories like, "I really wasn't looking to change
jobs, but they made me an offer I couldn't refuse!" Or the flip side
of this, "I told them I wanted that job so badly I would pay them!"
My own professional years, for the most part, have been spent in
television news where competition for jobs is fierce. When we do
win out over our competitors, those poor negotiators among us feel
compelled for want of a better word to "repay" our employer in
some way for the opportunity and we end up making far too many
concessions.

It is much more advantageous to adopt a psychological posture
that has the potential to reap better rewards. And it can be done. A
friend of mine named Karen Bryan is a secretary. She's thirtyish, has
a child with a learning disability, and is separated from her husband,
who has not been responsible in meeting his child support payments.
All in all, it was a time of upheaval for Karen when she moved from

Virginia to Denver, Colorado to begin a new life for herself and her child. For the next two and a half months, she looked for a job and met rejection after rejection. When she was at the point of not knowing how she was going to pay her rent, she finally got her first offer. From this point, she wins everlasting admiration. Instead of taking the offer at any price the employer was willing to pay, she negotiated. She told him her skills were worth $12,000 even though she knew the top of his range was around $10,500. She also told him she had other prospects on which she expected to be making a decision soon. She did have prospects, but she had no idea if they would come through. By maintaining a cool, calm, and confident demeanor externally, successfully camouflaging her internal nervousness, she completely psyched out the employer. He offered her $10,500. She looked dismayed and cast her eyes toward the floor. He offered $11,000. She accepted. The employer was ecstatic. He feels he is so lucky to have landed her for his staff—and he is.

Karen had only herself to rely on to make a living and she knew she had to have a fairly decent salary to be able to provide for her child. She doesn't appear to be saddled with the erroneous notion shared by many women that if you come into a job at a low salary, it won't be long until you will get a huge raise once they see how good you are. It doesn't work that way. Career consultant Hal Shook says, "Once you settle on a salary, that's it. You've had your chance. I think personally it is a very tough thing to overcome if you find out later that you are a few thousand dollars below par. About the only way you are going to get it is to go someplace else." Compensation director Gordy says, "The company is not going to throw the internal payroll out of whack." With this in mind, it should be easy to see that your big raise comes by negotiating before accepting a job.

Salary Compression

One of the most significant management problems today is the dilemma of how to handle new employees who are coming into positions at salaries not much below those who have been on the job for some time. This salary compression, as it is called, can create serious morale problems in business. Nevertheless, the newer employees may get raises more quickly than the long-term employees because the newer employees are more inclined to leave if raises aren't forthcoming.

Business recognizes money as a human motivator and human motivation produces profits. By the same token, companies will pay workers fifty cents an hour if allowed to, but companies also will pay valuable employees what they are worth if the employees do their part, effectively demanding that they are paid what they are worth.

You have to know your worth; forget everything but selling yourself and negotiating to get paid what you're worth or be satisfied with routine annual raises that trickle down. People who are taken advantage of usually let it happen to them. The responsibility to see that you are treated fairly begins with you. Management consultant Siegel says, "Market yourself. Learn more about the business. Go to school if necessary. Take advantage of all the opportunities in the company. As you become more valuable, negotiate for more pay. The best way to be thought of as a fool is to allow yourself to be underpaid. If you want to come up short, be shy, retiring, always work for others and forget about yourself." One thing for sure, women cannot coast because they see so many men who do less and get paid more. Women are proving themselves and even if it isn't fair—and it isn't—they generally have to be better to measure up. As somebody said, lucky that's not too difficult.

EIGHT

On-the-Job Negotiating

Negotiating Is Ongoing

The negotiating process goes on after you accept a job. "As soon as one of my clients accepts a job," says career consultant Ralph Minker, "we start the strategy for the next raise and promotion." While people are hired primarily because they do good jobs, they may not always be promoted because they do. You always hear that the basis for a successful negotiation is tied to performance, but the real basis is being able to sell or communicate that you have performed. You've got to let them know. No manager sits beside you for eight hours a day. Therefore, they don't know everything you do during your whole day. They know some things about you quicker than others. For instance, the news will spread rapidly if you made a huge blunder somewhere along the line, but, by and large, it is your responsibility to keep them informed about the things you want them to know about—your accomplishments.

You have to know who you are dealing with and how best to communicate with that person. Some people like to communicate orally; others prefer memos. You have to make yourself visible not only to your manager but to others in the organization. Other people need to know you, think well of you, and support you. Use some of your time during the first six months on a new job to meet people. Tell them you are new and you would like to know more about what they do for the company. They will be flattered that you are in-

terested and you, in the meantime, are learning about the organization. A person who is systematic about this will know more about
the interpersonal dynamics and the organizational dynamics at the
end of six months than many of their co-workers who have been
there for ten years.

Team versus Self-Interests

As you communicate your accomplishments and go about meeting
people, warns management consultant Sandra O'Connell, be careful
not to "become known as someone who is looking out solely for
yourself because that is as dysfunctional as not letting anybody
know about your accomplishments." It is a delicate line to follow in
letting people know what kind of job you are doing without coming
across as a person totally concerned with self-interests as opposed to
the corporate emphasis on the team. The most effective way to
communicate your successes is through a problem-solving context.
For example, if someone in the company tells you about a problem
and you offer suggestions on how to resolve it because you've been
successful in that area, then it becomes more of a case of volunteering information than patting yourself on the back. Or if someone at
a staff meeting says we need to figure out how to tackle the work
flow problem, you might say, "I'd be glad to take that on. I worked
with systems flow on my last job and with a little help, I think I can
find a solution." To communicate your skills in the best professional
light, use a problem-solving context that does not sound entirely inappropriate or make you look self-serving.

Visibility

One way to strengthen your negotiating position is to pay attention to your group skills. You would be astounded at how much
evaluation goes on at meetings. For instance, if you go to a meeting
as a member of a project team, you are exposed to other people
often at higher levels and from other departments. It is the best plat-
form from which to increase your visibility. People leave the meeting thinking or perhaps remarking to a co-worker, "Who is she? She
really had a sharp presentation. And did she ever ask some good

questions!" Or they comment to the contrary, "Did you hear that rambling report? I wouldn't want her in my department!" Women need to be attending meetings, speaking up, volunteering for task forces, and finding out which committees they might serve in the company. Ask, "Is there a meeting on this and is it appropriate for me to attend? What might I contribute?" A meeting can be an informal presentation of self and results.

By zeroing in on these aspects of your work environment, you are doing more for your future than you would be if you are focusing exclusively on a technical map of your work. One of the biggest things holding women back is that many of us see ourselves in a technical function such as a good programmer or a terrific writer. If we don't expand to grasp a broader perspective, then we are going to be stuck. There is a point, and it varies from company to company, when you have to go into management to get anywhere. And that means travel, longer hours, task forces, giving up technical skills, and accepting a much higher risk job. It is a decision that should be made consciously and deliberately. "It is fine if you want to continue with your technical position," says O'Connell, "but stop grousing about not having the salary that management has. You can't have it both ways."

Raise-Getting Strategies

Many of us remember the fruitless efforts Dagwood made in the comic strip as he tried to get a raise from Mr. Dithers. Unfortunately, many of our attempts aren't much more productive. When an employer plays on our emotions and says, "Who do you want to see fired in order for you to get a raise?" we don't know how to handle it. When an employer says there is no money in the budget, we believe what we hear. When an employer sidesteps a raise request by citing that company policy dictates that you can't get a raise at this time, we defer. Or when the employer tries to intimidate us by suggesting that other people are waiting in line for our jobs if we are not satisfied with our raises, we capitulate. Many of us have been sexually harassed in connection with raises and promotions, a subject that will be discussed shortly. And some of us don't ask for raises at all. Perhaps we don't take advancing ourselves as seriously as we do advancing the corporate agenda. With heightened awareness and negotiating knowledge these situations can be altered to have at least a less economically debilitating impact on us.

Performance Review

Most large and many small companies have standard forms for performance appraisal, and a performance review is a handy mechanism for you to turn to your benefit in negotiating higher raises and promotions. But as has been pointed out, the biggest flaw in the process is the lack of objective measurement. When someone says you are doing a good job, what does that mean? Say, "That's terrific to hear but I think it would help me to know specifically what you mean. Now here are the four main things I have been doing. Can you give me some examples of how you see my performance in these areas?" In some instances, a job performance standard is clearly spelled out. If you are a stock analyst and you don't return a predetermined percentage on your portfolio, then you haven't made it. Regardless of what your job is, you have to know how your performance is being measured in order to build a successful case for a raise.·

If the company you work for does not have a performance review set up, you should ask for one on an individual basis with your employer. Request it "because you appreciate his or her insight and you need the input to help you do your job better." The employer may reply, "Well, I'll meet with you from time to time to discuss your progress." You then say, "But I would like to be able to look over a specific period of time to see how I've been doing and how I can set goals for the future."

Keep a Job-Related Diary

Keep a running diary of work-related matters. If you haven't done that to date, perhaps your desk calendar can be used to help you recall events of the past few months. As you flip back through the weeks and months, much of what occurred at meetings noted on

	Employee's Name
Performance Appraisal Record	Position Title
	Supervisor's Name
	Position Title
	Period Covered from: to:

The primary prupose of this Performance Appraisal is employee performance improvement. Indicate the employee's major strengths, weaknesses and improvement opportunities/plans. Cite actual performance results or examples to support assessment. Avoid subjective assessments of the employee's promotability or potential to assume higher levels of responsibility.

Strengths

Weaknesses

Improvement Opportunities/Plans

Employee Signature	Date	**Note:** Signature indicates that this peformance appraisal has been reviewed with employee: it does not necessarily represent agreement. Employees are encouraged to discuss significant disagreements with supervisor's supervisor.
Supervisor Signature	Date	
Supervisor's Supervisor Signature	Date	

Performance Evaluation Record	Name		Page of
	Position Title		Position Code
	Operations		Department
	Division		Location

Using the space below, summarize performance results during the appraisal period in each area of major responsibility listing them in relative order of importance to attainment of unit and division goals. Discuss accomplishments in each area of responsibility separately. Be specific. Cite facts and figures whenever possible. Indicate whether performance exceeds, meets or does not meet requirements. Give reasons why performance exceeded or fell below expectations. Note when achievements were attained under particularly difficult circumstances.

Continued on Back Page

☐ TOO NEW TO RATE	Ratee's Signature	Date
☐ OUTSTANDING	Rater's Signature	Date
☐ SUPERIOR		
☐ GOOD	Reviewer's Signature	Date
☐ SATISFACTORY		
☐ MARGINAL	Personnel Signature	Date
☐ UNACCEPTABLE		

Improvements
Indicate below specific improvements to be made over the next appraisal period. It is also recommended that the time be taken to establish a timetable of specific events other than personal objectives to be accomplished over this period. These could be as the basis for the next evaluation. If space is insufficient, continue on separate sheet.

your calendar will come back to you. As a side note, the diary should be kept at home, not in the office. It is private and it is for you, if for no other reason than to supply material for your resume. Also keep a file of thank you letters or any correspondence commending or recognizing your abilities. Whatever favorable comments you can get in writing, do so. In addition to providing information that can strengthen your negotiating position for a higher raise, the material definitely documents a chain of events in case an employer calls you in to review something that happened six months ago. It's a way of getting blamed only for your own mistakes. This includes giving advice to superiors which they don't take. But most important, the log is excellent for you to use as you get ready for your performance appraisal.

Send a Memo

Since most companies have regular times when salary increases come up, you should know ahead of time when your performance review is scheduled. If your employer hasn't said anything, request an appointment to discuss your performance. However, Minker offers the very good suggestion that several days before the meeting you send a two- or three-page memo to the person who is going to conduct the review. You don't want it to sound padded or self-serving, but you will essentially be discussing three areas of your work: what you have been doing since your last review, what you anticipate for the future on your job, and what new knowledge you have acquired, that is, what you are doing to improve your skills.

In the memo, say something to the effect that you are looking forward to the review which is scheduled for next Wednesday. Mention that you have your notes of the last six months or for whatever period of time has elapsed since the last review and you have outlined for yourself how you see your performance and how you see the future developing. Then say, "I thought you might like an advance copy." What you are doing is helping the other person to help you. You recognize that no supervisor has a day-to-day account of what you do and you are acknowledging that he or she has other responsibilities of supervision that extend beyond you. And you are gearing the memo to bringing the employer up-to-date on you in your own carefully chosen words.

List your duties and emphasize your achievements and contributions over the past few months. The work you do is not trivial. You want the employer to know and to remember and to be impressed with the complexity, the quantity, and perhaps the level of what you have been handling, as well as your results. The employer will want to know what contributions you are making which are of benefit to the company and your manager. If you are one of a team that does well, it makes your employer look good also.

The second section of the memo is usually smaller and may come under a heading like "career advancement." Tell the employer if you have taken some course in the evening or if you have attended some work-related workshop or seminar. Quite likely you have assumed new responsibilities over the past few months which have resulted in personal development. Indicate what job-oriented books you have read or what cassette series you have taken home for study. All this suggests that your mind is growing and you understand that the best way for you to be your best is to continue to study and the best way to be of help to the organization or your manager is to continue to study and improve and apply it.

The third part of the memo can be called "some ideas I would like to discuss." These are couched in terms of goals. Thus the performance review becomes oriented toward goal-setting for the future, rather than nit-picking about the past. What you write in your memo is based on solid facts, but you are suggesting that it is time for you to assume new responsibilities. You might volunteer or raise the question of helping your supervisor on some project. You might draw attention to additional training you would like to undertake in order to equip yourself for advancement. It may be setting your eyes on a particular position at some point in the future. What you are doing in this part of the memo is alerting the employer to your goals, getting him or her to endorse your ideas and recognize your enthusiasm. You are also making it easy for him or her to appreciate the fact that you are a strong member of the team and you are including your employer as an ally in some of your long-range plans.

Performance Monitoring

When making out this outline, you are reviewing yourself, asking "What have I done?" And if you have failed on a project or two, this may not be the time to talk about any big-time plans for the future. Instead, address how you might do better in the coming months and produce at least a faint ray of evidence that some progress is already taking place. Express enthusiasm. Part of the reason for keeping a diary is so that you can monitor your own performance. As you look back over the week or the month or the year, you should be able to see patterns. "I've neglected something or here is a problem that keeps coming up and I'm not handling it as well as I should. Maybe I need to take some training or ask for some assistance in order to deal with it. Otherwise, this little flaw may keep me from realizing my full potential or from being given a bigger raise."

Whenever there is a roadblock, look at it as a problem to be solved rather than an immovable object. If you see a roadblock and management sees a roadblock, how can you get around it? It may require special training. Not everybody is willing to go to evening classes two or three nights a week to overcome an obstacle. However, some are, and that makes the difference. So partly your own base commitment to furthering yourself and the realization that you are going to have to be more than an eight-hour a day worker are forerunners to advancement. You have to do more than what is expected. Most job descriptions address the average person. Those who are promoted and rise rapidly are the ones who regularly and enthusiastically go beyond minimum expectations of the job.

By the time you send your memo, a specific time and date should be scheduled for your appraisal. By considering little things like interview timing, you maximize your possibility of success. If you can control when the meeting will take place, do it. Friday afternoons are out. The employer may want to leave a bit earlier for the weekend. Monday mornings are bad when mail is stacked to the roof. A mid-week morning is probably the best time. If the employer wants to see you at 9:00 Monday morning, say you have an appointment at that time (or something important going on) and suggest

Tuesday or Wednesday at the same hour. Certainly don't treat your raise request as something so light it can be cleared up on the elevator ride to lunch. And don't discuss the matter with co-workers. Go about your work without precipitating a whirlwind of activity in the days prior to your review which might reflect unfavorably on your credibility as you discuss your performance with your employer. Do, however, try to foster a genuine climate of good will with your manager. It is never advantageous to negotiate in a hostile atmosphere. Salary negotiations can be every bit as delicate as SALT talks with the Russians. Until you learn the delicacy of the situation, err on the side of caution. Success often depends on subtle factors like the employer's feelings, background, and attitudes about women as well as the personality of the company itself. Is it conservative, established, old, or young? What is the image projected? Each woman must use her own best judgment in molding this advice to fit her own unique situation.

Negotiation Feedback

Once in the performance review meeting, you can help keep the atmosphere amicable by reminding yourself that negative feedback is not to be interpreted as a personal attack on you.

The curious thing about a number of managers, though, is that they have a great deal of difficulty giving negative feedback in the first place. No matter what your level, it is difficult for a manager to say you are not measuring up. Martin-Marietta's John Gordy says, "This may be the biggest weakness among managers. It takes guts to sit down and say you are not cutting it and here are the reasons why. It is much easier to say you are doing a fine job and here's your raise."

Management consultant O'Connell, a specialist in management-employee communications, says one of the reasons some managers have a hard time criticizing is because they tend to verbalize the negative feedback in ways that attack the person rather than the job. For example, a bad manager might say, "That was a lousy job you did on that last assignment!" On the other hand, a manager who is a little more sensitive to communication techniques might say instead to an employee whose writing is not up to standard, "That last assignment just did not have all the pertinent data in it. The budget for this year was omitted and no summary was included. And the language seemed more suitable for our internal accountants than for our client." By making specific references to the job, it is easier for the manager to discuss shortcomings with the employee and it is easier for the employee to handle also. There is no doubt that you are addressing a job-related issue and the language tends to be less personal and less subjective, which in turn reduces conflict, hostility, and defensiveness.

It is not uncommon for many of us to translate a discussion of on-the-job weaknesses into self-criticism. We don't say, "What do I need to do differently?" We think, "What is wrong with me?" If you are being criticized in a performance review and you find it upsetting, here are some strategies to help you get on top of the matter. Calmly ask for examples. Say, "I want to improve but it is not clear to me exactly what you mean. It would help if you would give me some examples." Obviously you won't be helping communications if you say, "Well, if you don't give me examples, how do you expect me to do what you say!" Other tension-reducing phrases you might want to use are "Perhaps you may not have had this information available . . ." or "I don't imagine our differences are very far apart."

It's Crying Time

If you find negative feedback upsetting to the point you think you may cry, say, "This comes as a surprise to me and I'm finding it difficult to assess at this moment. I know that if I have some time, I will be able to come back and work with you on how to improve that facet of my performance. Could we meet again tomorrow?" Make it clear that you are not going off angry, rather that it will be better for the job results if you return tomorrow.

To keep from crying in stressful situations has been a tremendous problem for me, as it is for many women. And as I mentioned earlier, there's no place for that kind of emotionalism in a negotiation—not so much because of the effect it might have on the employer, but because of the effect it has on you. By allowing your emotions to take over, you can't possibly be thinking clearly. Thereby, you can't negotiate, since by its very nature, negotiating requires you to be somewhat detached and analytical. Crying is a sign of loss of control. It is analogous to what some men do in the work environment—explode in anger. Both emotions represent inappropriate business behavior, although they are not thought of in the same way. Men are seldom penalized for exploding, and in some cases they may be rewarded. Women, on the other hand, are never rewarded for crying. It's a no-win situation. The time to deal with the potentiality of tears is before you reach the point where it is uncontrollable. When you first begin to feel upset, start telling yourself you can handle this, try to relax as we've already discussed, and if all else fails, excuse yourself before the tidal wave hits. But I must say that the more experience you gain and the confidence that comes with a few successes diminish the probability of tears proportionately—at least, they did for me.

Most women today would do anything rather than cry at a business meeting, and the steps some of them take to control tears are worth repeating. One woman became known as "more hardnosed" than any of the men because she would get a stern look on her face and abruptly leave the room when things took a turn for the worse. Her abruptness was interpreted among her colleagues as a "no-nonsense approach," but nobody followed her to the restroom where she cried until she gained her composure. Another woman keeps a spare bottle of an allergy medicine in her purse and fakes an "attack" whenever she feels it is impossible to keep from crying. She actually sprayed her eyes once to have an excuse for the tears already there. And I suppose more than one has whipped out dark glasses claiming doctor's orders to counter a minor eye irritation.

There are women who see this issue differently, though. They feel men and women would be better off if they could display their emotions openly. Whether you allow yourself to cry or not may depend on your relationship with your manager. If you feel comfortable with him or her, some advise you to let your emotions go for a few minutes. They say it is not the worst thing that can happen to you. I agree with that, but by the same token, it is not the best thing that can happen either. A senior vice president of a large corporation was asked how he views a woman who cries in a business setting and he said, "as less effective than if she hadn't."

One woman supervisor reported that a man on her staff cried during a performance review. She said she sat quietly until he pulled himself together. Perhaps the world will have advanced when women and men cry together in the board room, but this state of emotionalism and openness is still "cry in the sky."

Negotiate as an Equal Adult

Author Alice Sargent asserts in her research that women often assume the child role with a male employer. This can be particularly evident in a negotiating situation. The employer becomes the father figure and the woman assumes the role of a child. Sometimes it works in reverse. Female secretaries and managers may treat men who work for or with them as sons. Regardless, the point being made is that there is little adult-to-adult communication between women and men in the job market. Part of the reason underlying this theory is that we have so few models for adult-to-adult communications. About the only way men and women communicate adult-to-adult is when they are lovers (and sometimes not even then). It is suggested that the sexual anxiety in a work environment causes people to seek the parent and child roles in order to accomplish transactions.

These thoughts are brought home in this story relayed to me by Sandra O'Connell. "A woman in one of my workshops told me that every time she went in to ask for a raise, she came away without one. When the transaction was analyzed, it became clear that the employer had assumed the role of father figure and the woman was playing the role of the ungrateful child. He would say things to her like 'Well, we sent you to that nice conference in New York. Look at all we have done for you and we are doing other things for you too.' I asked her, 'Was that explained to you as part of the compensation package? Is that something they do not do for men?' 'Oh no,' said the woman, 'the men get all that.' 'Well, why is he saying that is an extra?' She said, 'That's what my father did to me. How can you be so ungrateful?' Once we sorted out what he was doing to her, whether deliberately or not, we figured out ways for her to break out of that. I encouraged her to adopt the adult mode, which is descriptive, uses descriptive language, asks questions, includes data to analyze and not being caught in the trap of acting like a guilty little girl or an ungrateful child." Women need to learn the limits of their role as employee and the limits of the employer's authority. When we do, such remarks as "We just sent you to that nice conference" won't stump us. In fact, they won't be said at all and statements like that certainly don't deserve a reply. It only legitimizes them.

Make Them Want to Reward You

Some companies call employees in without prior notice, hand you a letter indicating a raise, congratulate you, and you're out the door. Initially, this impersonal system doesn't appear to leave much room for negotiating, but there is room. If you know your company does this and about at what intervals, it is especially important that you ask for an appointment to discuss your performance with your manager during the time he or she is making decisions about raises. Also, provide him or her with the "memo" in advance of your scheduled meeting. Now at least you have had input into this mechanized process and you've laid the groundwork for a bigger raise by talking firsthand about what you are doing for the company. You may not ever specifically talk about money, but you have set the employer up to want to reward you, rather than thinking, "Oh, what do we have to give her to keep her reasonably happy?" Instead of perhaps a 5 percent or a 7 percent raise, you may get a 10 or 12 percent or an even higher increase.

It is not a good idea to put a specific dollar request on paper. Such a tactic may seem hard or unbending and has a tendency to come across as an ultimatum. That doesn't have to be the case in a conversation, but again, the key word is flexibility. You might want to suggest a bonus as an alternative because sometimes managers find it easier to give a bonus incentive in place of a flat salary increase (here's that salary compression problem again). Some companies don't give bonuses but many do. Bonuses are tied to performance and you've built your case entirely on merit and production, not because you have the same number of years of service as so and so.

Translate Accomplishments into Dollars

The hard part of negotiating comes when we have to translate goals and accomplishments into dollars. What is your cue to move from one to the other now that the employer is conditioned to want to reward you? When the employer says something like "You're one of my most valuable people," or "I wish I had a hundred like you," or "You're the best," then that is a natural steppingstone to ask the question about how this might be translated to your income. It is better, of course, if the employer makes the transition for you. At least 50 percent of the time you may not discuss actual dollars at all. By carefully preparing your memo and arranging for a performance review, you are essentially getting the employer in the right frame of mind so that he or she will want to give you a top raise. The employer may or may not indicate exactly what your raise will be during your meeting.

On the other hand, if you are in an especially strong position on your job and perhaps your management doesn't seem to be quite as responsive as it might be, say "One other question I would like to talk about is salary." Relating to your performance and value to the company, ask "How is this translated to salary?" And then wait for an answer. Let the employer fill any dead air. If he or she has some hesitation and brings up the old argument that everybody at Grade 11 gets the same, then inquire about an incentive bonus. Salespersons do it all the time, but again, success is more difficult to measure for some types of jobs. At this point, the rapport, the human relationship, and the flow of communications with your employer are extremely important.

Testing the "Tried and True"

Sometimes we are thwarted in our efforts for a bigger raise when the company cites inflation as the villain: "We have to hold costs to a minimum and I can't go beyond our ceiling. It's company policy." The rationale behind a ceiling can seem faulty. If a salesperson sells 100 more cars because of a raise incentive, you may have a ceiling, but that person certainly is producing more than the raise costs. If your employer resists your request because of company policy on a ceiling, it may suggest that he or she is weak and unable to press for more even when it is justified, "Well, the president of the company says these are the guidelines and there will be no more discussions between you and me about it."

There are managers out there who are inept in the interpersonal communications required of first-class management. Many companies are aware of this and are becoming more sensitive to how managers are selected. Traditionally, a first-line manager has been the best technician in the place. Now it is beginning to be understood that the best underwriter or programmer may not make the best manager. Business is also getting a little more sophisticated about providing the training, coaching, and tools that are going to be required from managers in the future.

Nevertheless, when a manager says your raise is set by company policy on wage guidelines, there are ways to diplomatically test the policy. One principle of negotiating is not accepting everything that is said to you as being carved in stone. You have to realize that from the company's point of view, the "company policy" argument is a good business tactic to keep down its costs, and that includes your salary. You might say that you are "only asking for your fair market value as demonstrated by your performance and even the President of the United States doesn't want people to be paid less than they are worth." Or you might say, "You mean no changes can be made, not even in emergencies?" The employer is likely to concede that only in extreme emergencies could the policy be altered. Proceed with your request which is important enough to fall in that category. Or you might want to use a tactic that was illustrated earlier. Negotiate down for less work. If you stop working extra hours, then somebody will have to be paid to take up the slack. The employer may decide it might as well be you.

Probably the best use of the "company policy" position among managers is made when employees ask for raises at times other than the annual review. It is true that management is not prepared to constantly change salaries every week or every month. A system is needed in business to help plan and estimate costs against income. But the big benefit accrued to management from an annual review policy is to keep raise-seeking employees off its back for eleven months of the year. There may be times when you will want to or should request a raise at a time other than at performance review time. For example, if you have just been assigned a large chunk of a departing employee's workload in addition to your own normal responsibilities, then that constitutes a valid and immediate reason for extra compensation. If you have just scored a spectacular success that is widely commended, then you should ask to have that turned into higher earnings. Don't wait until the excitement has died down. Strike while the iron is hot.

Another Job Offer

Of course, another job offer is the superlative position from which to negotiate a raise at any time of the year. If you are prepared to take the new job, go to your employer and tell him or her that you have an interesting offer. Give the reasons why it is appealing and why it challenges you, including the salary. Say you have a few days to make your decision and, out of courtesy, you wanted him or her to know. Continue along the vein that some loose ends need to be taken care of and because you are conscientious, you are prepared to help arrange for a transition. Sometimes you might even volunteer to come in on Wednesday nights for a month and Saturday mornings for a while after you take the new job. Next say, "I've enjoyed being here. I've felt a sense of reward while contributing to what we are doing at this company, a sense of teamwork, and I've respected your leadership. I suppose I really would be interested in staying right here and following through on what we've started, if there was a way to make it as financially rewarding for me." Now the employer has a chance to make a bid for you.

If you are anticipating a firm job offer but it hasn't come through yet, you might want to "tease" the employer by mentioning the possibility of employment elsewhere. But don't invent such teases. Say something along these lines, "I was having lunch today with an old college classmate when her employer joined us for a few minutes. Before he left, he suggested that he would like to talk to me about an opening in the company. I'm not taking the incident too seriously, but the whole thing caught me by surprise. At least, it is nice to know that one of our competitors has an interest in what I do." The employer is getting the message. You may be stolen because your present management is not doing enough to keep you happy. If your manager values what you do, the word will reach whomever it needs to reach. Don't use legitimate teases often or in a threatening, ultimatum manner, but more as an interesting bit of information that came up in an unexpected way.

The No-Money Plea

Another argument used to keep raises low is the "no money" plea, which we discussed earlier in this chapter. Career consultant Bill Devries sees this tactic as a "put off kind of thing" or avoidance tactic employers use to discourage nonperformers. However, it can also be used to divert good performers who don't have negotiating skills. As Pfizer divisional vice president Max Hughes says, "The more agreeable persons tend to be imposed upon." If you have read the company's annual financial report, you know whether more money is being made this year than last.

Others Aren't Getting Raises

Employers also like to use this tactic: "Others in the department are doing good jobs and they are not getting big raises." The best thing to do is give him or her an all-knowing look square in the eye and say nothing. That is the manager's problem. Let him or her solve it. If you don't think you can carry that off, say, "I am only talking about myself, but certainly anybody who does good work should be rewarded." If the employer pursues a comparison of you and others, something you don't want to initiate, recall some of the superlatives he or she might have used in the performance review to praise your work which sets you aside from the rest. Or emphasize yourself the qualities that make you stand out.

One of the best ways to qualify for the maximum possible raise, of course, is to expand your duties. Take on extra assignments, broaden your job description, and thereby give your manager positive backup reasons to reward you. More often than not, your duties have expanded considerably since you were hired whether or not you've noticed.

Keep Abreast of Business

In some instances, your raise request can be tied to keeping abreast of business. For example, the *Wall Street Journal* reports from time to time what the average salary increase is. If the publication indicates that the average professional salary rose last year by 9 percent and breaks the figures down to individual industries, all you have to do is compare the national average to your last raise. If you got only a 5 percent increase, this suggests that you may want to negotiate a bigger raise. Management, no doubt, realizes that if people in other companies around town are giving twice as much in increases, then employees are going to be thinking about shifting companies. If you are a productive worker, even an inept supervisor will want to discuss a raise as opposed to interviewing, hiring, and training another person, someone who may not work out as well as you.

The most natural thing for an employer to do when faced with a raise request is to delay a decision on the matter. During the negotiating session, you will want to do your utmost to get a decision on the spot; at the very least, try to put a time limit on the answer. If the employer says he or she needs more time to think about your request, set up a follow-up meeting within the next couple of days.

If you have given your employer the best possible explanation of why you are worth a top raise, and he or she doesn't hold out much hope that it will be granted, or if you feel you have been unfairly denied a raise, ask the manager if he or she would appeal your case to a higher authority in the company. As a last resort and only as a last resort, you can appeal a raise decision yourself. Preface either of these actions by saying to your employer, "I know you are just executing guidelines set forth by the company and I appreciate the position you are in, but I do think I have valid reasons why I should be exempted from that standard at this time. I would like to appeal my case on that basis."

If you handle it this way, the manager shouldn't see it as a downgrading of himself or herself. However, if the route for such an appeal is through the personnel office, many of those in the career consulting field don't hold out prospects of much success. Minker says, "Personnel people are non-negotiators. You do not talk salary, get promoted faster or get better raises, by and large, when you deal with personnel departments. The corporate treasurer is the one who knows where the money is."

When to Avoid a Raise Request

About the only times a raise request should positively be ruled out are if you just got a raise five weeks ago or if you've learned the company is facing imminent takeover! Remember, the bigger raises do not go to the employee who quietly toils in the background and makes no concerted effort to increase her income. Quite the contrary. Those who make an assertive and strategic campaign for higher earnings are the ones who get the better salaries. You may not always get as big a raise as you would like, but odds are it is bigger than you would have received had you not set out deliberately to translate your accomplishments into a higher income.

When you get your raise, thank your employer and reassure him or her that he or she has done the right thing. Later, formalize the raise agreement in writing by sending a note to her or him.

Regardless of your raise-getting strategies, it is a good idea to keep both feet in the job market. Scarcity of jobs can ward off your making rash demands and, on the other hand, the knowledge that others are interested in you is the best source of confidence and negotiating power.

NINE

Out-of-Bounds Negotiating: Sexual Harassment

What Is Sexual Harassment?

Someone once asked a policewoman the following question: "If a co-worker asked for sexual relations and you refused, how many times would it have to happen before you considered it sexual harassment?" She answered, "He can ask all he wants if he's not in a position to threaten my job!" Unfortunately, many sexual harassers are in just that position. A study conducted among federal workers found that 67 percent of alleged sexual harassment offenders were supervisors—either line managers, division heads, or administrators who had power to determine raises and promotions. Representative James Hanley, who chaired the House hearings on sexual harassment in the federal government in late 1979, says, "Our preliminary investigation has shown that the problem is not only epidemic; it is pandemic—an everyday, everywhere occurrence." And indications are that the situation is no better in the private sector. The lowest estimates of the percentage of working women who have experienced sexual harassment are in the range of 70 percent.

The U. S. Office of Personnel Management defines sexual harassment to include deliberate or repeated unsolicited verbal comments, gestures, or physical contact of a sexual nature which are unwelcome and interfere with an employee's job performance. A supervisor who uses implicit or explicit coercive sexual behavior to control, influence, or affect the career, salary, or job of an employee is engaging in sexual harassment. As I heard one woman say, "Sexual harassment is something 80 percent of women would agree on. When it happens to you, you know it."

As you might suspect, a large gray area of sexual interchanges is used to cloud the issue of sexual harassment and often detracts from the more serious abuses taking place on the job. What one woman might consider harassing behavior would go unnoticed by another woman. But sexual harassment, for the most part, is not minor infractions such as a wink or some other mild flirtation that we get on a daily basis. Sexual harassment is verbal and physical action that people would generally agree to be inappropriate. Dr. Nancy Felipe Russo of the American Psychological Association says, "There is solid evidence of intimidation and direct threats of physical force and it doesn't matter whether the woman is disabled or ugly by the standards of beauty in our society. Women get sexually harassed and if they complain about it, they get punished for it. That's clear."

An Environment Conducive to Negotiating

A major component of negotiating success is having a working environment that is conducive to negotiating success. If women have to negotiate with an employer who has inappropriate, one-dimensional attitudes toward women, as sexual harassers do, you can't relate to him with the professional dignity required of a first-rate negotiator. And once on the job, you can't negotiate for raises and promotions based on your professional skills and abilities if you are subjected to unfair abuse of power through sexual harassment. This has nothing to do with social interactions or relationships freely entered into by employees.

Improving the workplace for women so that they can apply negotiating skills without an undue handicap can come from focusing much-needed attention on the subject of sexual harassment. It is important that women have forums to talk about the issue with other women and that men and women talk about it together. No one knows for sure whether there is more harassment going on now or less after recent attention paid to the subject. But if I had to guess, I would say less. The national publicity generated and the worthwhile efforts under way in local areas are taking the issue out of the closet. Once sexual harassment is being discussed in the open, offenders and victims alike will realize that such behavior is intolerable, not to mention illegal. Only then can the working environment have fewer harassers and more negotiators.

It's an Economic Problem

Although some tend to see this as a social problem for women, it is a problem that has a profound economic impact as well. The research of Lin Farley, author of *Sexual Shakedown*, indicates that whenever there is a high rate of sexual harassment, there is a corresponding high rate of female resignations and job losses. Testimony before the House hearings proved that career advancement is often impeded by sexual harassment and that the pervasiveness and general acceptance of sexual harassment circumscribe women's employment opportunities in every respect. The women hurt worst by this are those who can least afford it—those with limited options to pursue when their jobs are in jeopardy.

The "Boys Will Be Boys" Attitude

The prevailing attitude of management has been "boys will be boys." Offices exist where sexual harassment is "standard operating procedure." The victims frequently are afraid and embarrassed to complain publicly, since such complaints might make them the object of retaliation by the employer and sometimes even the object of ridicule from other women in the office. One woman complained of sexual harassment and apparently had enough documentation to convince higher-ranking officials in the company that she had a legitimate grievance. The company's action was to promote the offender out of the office. He was handed not only a better job but more pay. The woman, in the meantime, was ostracized by her co-workers as being a troublemaker. Both male and female employees believed she must have done something to bring about his advances.

Women's Support Groups

A change of thinking is required on this issue. Until recently, women found themselves isolated among co-workers who didn't want to get involved. But signs suggest we may be growing beyond this as more and more support groups develop. Women who have begun to talk among themselves have found that other women are being harassed by the same man. There is safety in numbers when women band together. Carol Pitts, who conducts sexual harassment workshops primarily in Washington, D. C., says she sees the time when women in an organization will ask top management to encourage discussion and training for men whose behavior needs to be worked on.

Enforcing the Law

This problem for women exists partly because management allows it to exist. The beginning of the end of the problem will be evident when top managers start sending down clear, forceful directives forbidding such conduct. They will do this quicker when more employees—both male and female—demand it.

Title VII of the 1964 Civil Rights Act prohibiting sex discrimination is just the first of a developing body of laws that protects women from sexual harassment. The Equal Employment Opportunity Commission has taken the position that sexual harassment violates Title VII and complaints can be filed with that arm of government. The EEOC rules give the Commission the right to grant backpay awards, reinstate employees, order their promotions, or apply any other type of relief available under the civil rights law. If an employer in either the public or private sector refuses to settle a complaint outside of court, EEOC can pursue the case in federal courts. When costs for legal fees and damages start cutting into company profits, we will see bold directives banning the behavior.

Directives against sexual harassment should be distributed to every employee and posted for all to see. Sexual harassment should be broadly defined and the employees should be made aware that this activity is illegal. These directives should set forth the steps the employee must take to file a discrimination complaint and emphasize that retaliation is prohibited. Finally, it should be made known that employees who harass can expect swift and stern disciplinary action. Coupled with directives, however, should be training sessions for managers. For example, role playing exercises can demonstrate harassing behavior. Consequently, a heightened awareness can help managers spot harassing tendencies in lower-ranking managers within their jurisdiction. Training is the key to prevention. Handling sexual harassment after the fact is extremely difficult. The process of filing a complaint and the amount of time it takes to process one is too long. The problem has to be resolved ultimately through training programs. Without dialogue on the subject as part of the training, a harasser is going to look at the directive on the bulletin board and say, "This doesn't apply to me."

Personal versus Professional Relationships

The ironic element in all of this is that women have been conditioned to be flattered by many suggestive comments and actions even though they may not like the man proferring them. On the other hand, some men don't realize their behavior is harassing. They may be behaving the way they think a man is expected to behave. Although this story addresses the less serious sexual comments, it points up a working environment that undermines women. A woman said that in her office the men always relate to their female co-workers on a personal level and not as professionals. Every morning it would be "Don't you look sexy today!" Or "You really look great in that sweater!" Finally, when one of the more guilty offendders said it one time too many, she looked at him and firmly said, "Why can't you simply say hello. I don't appreciate hearing those ridiculous comments every day. How would you like it if I treated you as a person without a mind?" The man sincerely apologized. He had been behaving in the way he thought was acceptable office behavior. For that office and many others, it was acceptable and still is.

The hardcore harassers, though, are those people who manipulate and use power over everyone they can. Sex is one weapon that is available for them to control those who depend on them for jobs, raises, and promotions. Since men are in most of the power positions, sexual harassment is an abuse of power that most often has an adverse effect on women and, to a lesser extent, homosexuals.

What's a Woman to Do?

In the meantime, what's a woman to do? Some have tried humor to ward off unwanted attention. This only encourages the harasser to try again. Others have resigned themselves to the fact that sexual innuendos and intimate pats go with the territory of work. They try to ignore them as much as possible. This kind of denial also doesn't work very well. Others have tried turning the tables. A woman I know said she got so tired of the sexual suggestions of an employer that once when she was in his office and he again made some explicit remark, she stared him down and said, "OK, deliver! Right now, here on the desk!" He backed down.

Not many women could have carried that off. We often have an irrational fear of being seen as pushy, bitchy, or aggressive. Sometimes that fear is so overwhelming that some women feel they are going to "lose their femininity." What happens is that they go out of their way to act submissively or docilely. We're afraid to trust our own intuitions. We think "Oh, he couldn't have possibly meant what he said." If you determine that the man means more than a mild office flirtation and you're not interested, a clear and early signal to that effect is called for.

When something offensive happens to you on the job, senior staff assistant Rosemary Storey of the House Subcommittee on Investigations, which conducted the sexual harassment hearings, advises you to handle it this way: "Excuse me, Mr. Smith, but I don't appreciate that kind of a remark. I find it inappropriate and I wish you would stop it immediately." She says you have to "nip it in the bud." Then, if your treatment gets worse and you decide to complain formally, you'll have a much better case. You can see how your position would be strengthened this way rather than by saying, "I tried to laugh it off for six months until I couldn't stand it anymore." Don't let things go so long you feel you have to walk out. A much better approach is to firmly let the harasser know the first time he tries anything that this is not what you expect on the job.

Another thing a woman can do is turn to someone else in the office and say "Did you hear him say that?" Or "Did you see him do that?" Get it on the record. If you have to bring a grievance, then you have some witnesses to call in.

Finally, when this kind of situation starts developing, take notes. This can be used later as evidence. Women for the most part are not attuned to this. Sexual harassment often occurs when and where there are no witnesses. Your best protection is to immediately write down what you said and what he said. It will help your case if it comes to that.

A Misuse of Power

Sexual harassment, as has already been pointed out, is basically a misuse of power by those in higher positions against those in lower-level jobs—usually women. But now that women are moving into nontraditional fields where men are their equals or subordinates, are these women being sexually harassed? Some women are, some aren't, and some turn out to be harassers themselves. Dr. Gloria Harris says she has met many successful and attractive women in her management training courses who claim they have never been sexually harassed.

Some women entering nontraditional jobs find themselves objects of a different kind of harassment. They are being attacked as being "frustrated" or "not being a real woman," as the milder descriptions put it. One story told to me along these lines was by a woman who was giving a three-day lecture series on women at a high school in New York State. During a break she walked into the lunchroom where a number of men were gathered eating lunch. One large man walked toward her. (Wouldn't you know it? He was the football coach.) He started to make sexual remarks that weren't aimed directly at the woman but as asides to the other men. She proceeded to eat her sandwich quietly. He kept it up while she did her best to ignore him. When she got up to leave, he said, "Hey you, why don't you come back an hour early tomorrow and I'll fix your problem!"

For the first time since entering the room, she looked directly at him and said, "Why an hour? I think a couple of minutes ought to do it." The other men in the room burst into hoots of laughter. A challenge to his masculinity was the worst retribution she could have given him. Nevertheless, attacking a person in kind provides no real progress. Casting aspersions on a person's sexuality has been a tool some men have used, but one women have been reluctant to use. And I hope they keep on being reluctant to use it. It only heightens hostility and blocks any meaningful education that might help men and women communicate in the marketplace.

Women as Harassers?

I listened in amazement as a friend of mine, a charming, attractive man, told me that women have harassed him. I asked, "How do you handle it when it happens?" He said, "Oh, not very well. I don't recall a single discussion in my whole life on how to turn it down." Could this be true? Do women harass too? Dr. Russo says, "Insofar as we are talking about power...you will find people of either sex using every tool at their disposal for the manipulation of others and women are no more pure or less pure than men." But Dr. Gloria Harris, a behavioral psychologist, says she doesn't expect harassment by females to be widespread. Women, she says, "are not conditioned to pursue, they are conditioned to flee." She also says she is angry because her insurance practice rates keep going up as a result of sexual harassment charges levied against male therapists. Harris recollects only one female therapist being charged and she thinks the ratio of male versus female therapists who are also harassers is analogous to the rest of the workplace where women are in positions of power.

Using Sex to Get Better-Paying Jobs

What about women who use sex to negotiate themselves into better-paying jobs? Does it happen often and are they successful? A woman who conducts sexual harassment workshops said, "We had a workshop where a woman said out loud . . . that she used sex to move up the ladder. People went berserk!" Another woman said, "Sometimes the trick is just to get out of the secretarial pool. There were women with some ability who used sex to get a head start and then they were off and running. I've seen it happen."

On this aspect of out-of-bounds negotiating, Anne Turpeau who chairs the Sexual Harassment Task Force for the Washington, D. C., Commission for Women, says, "What I take exception to is when a woman prostitutes herself to get ahead. It is clearly a money proposition. Either the increases in salary, the better pay or whatever... I have been in the job market long enough to have seen it." I don't doubt that her assessment is correct, but I tend to think for every woman who uses sex successfully as one of her negotiating tools to get better job-related rewards, there are scores who may have tried it and found themselves out on the street without jobs. In sexual conquests, men gain points among male peers and women lose points. Women's credibility among co-workers is severely diminished, and if friction develops within her liaison, she, not he, is the one who most often ends up job hunting.

In all fairness here, I think that most women who enter into sexual relations on the job do it for romantic notions and not for cold, hard, calculative reasons. But since the man is usually in a higher position, the betterment of her lot is probably implicit in the arrangement. At this point, I will give you the most useless advice ever given because it is the most unheeded advice: If you want to ensure yourself of maximum negotiating potential as you move upward, keep your personal relations separate from your business dealings. It is just one more mark of professionalism, and women need every edge they can get . . .within bounds, of course.

Unsettling Work Environment

Because of the massive influx of women in the job market and rapidly changing roles, the present work environment is unsettling and confusing for men and women. We are going through a period of reshuffling and reassessment. If we are ever to achieve equality in the marketplace, this upheaval is an inevitable part of it. Eventually, what works and what doesn't work will be clear. Perhaps by then the nature of working conditions will have changed so that sex won't be confused with power, peer pressure will dictate that sexual harassment is taboo, and at last we'll have a standard for what is appropriate office behavior for men and women who are equals.

TEN

The Image of A Negotiator

The Smiling, Amenable Cookie Giver

I come from a long line of smiling people. In the good times, the men smiled and the women smiled. In the bad times, the men stopped but the women went right on smiling. That smile was a pacifying trait everyone expected of women.

As a child it was easy for me to classify my relatives: some always gave me cookies, but there were others I couldn't be sure about. Those who looked less approachable and more standoffish kept me off balance. I didn't impose on them nearly so often and when they gave me cookies, I appreciated them because they were harder to come by. My favorites were those who smiled a lot. They were nicer to be around and they always gave me cookies. They would say, "Now this is the last cookie you can have" and they would smile as they handed it to me. Then I knew if I really wanted another cookie, I could have.

The moral to all this: Don't let the other person in a negotiation find out you're a smiling, amenable cookie giver. You'll lose. Personally, I'm trying to replace my smile with the Clint Eastwood squint, but I'm not having much luck.

How People Perceive Us

How other people perceive us is fundamental to the art of negotiating, and perceptions are largely within our control. Powerful men
through the ages have known this and have paid scrupulous attention
to details of their mannerisms, bearing, and dress in a conscious
effort to maximize their potential. It's also an awareness women
have long had in their personal lives, but one they're just beginning
to tap in the business world. You may have expert negotiating skills,
but the effectiveness and force of those skills will fail unless the
other person's perception of you matches the words you are saying.
Further, the full merit of your accomplishments can go unrecognized
if the aura that comes from you defeats your own best interests.
Within 30 seconds of a first meeting, the other person draws all kinds
of conclusions about you, conclusions that generally stick. You've
had little chance other than to say "Hello, how are you?" and you're
tagged for better or worse. The thing to do is get tagged for better,
and you can do it.

I don't like the word "image." Its current fad use connotes a
triumph of style over substance. That's the last thing I want to promote. I think of the concept of image or another's perception of
us solely as a vehicle to help support substance. Bluntly, the sub-
stantive qualities about you shouldn't be disregarded because others
perceive things about you that detract from substance.

Know When You're Conducting Business and When You're Not

The subject of image is a particularly difficult area for working
women. We have so few role models to look to for guidance on what
does and doesn't work. What bits and pieces of the picture we've
pieced together still have to stand the test of time. Many are still grap-
pling with conflicts stemming from behavioral patterns prescribed
for women in our upbringing, patterns that aren't working in the
business world. Some want to succeed but actually have an irrational
fear that it might happen. These internal conflicts have to be resolved
before a solid, impressive image can come through of women who
know who they are and where they are going.

It is my impression that many women could be projecting more positive images if they would change their "either/or" mindset. These internal conflicts seem to persist in many cases because women feel their only alternative is to be 100 percent "all business" forever, and they're hesitant to make that commitment. A better way to look at it is simply to know when you are conducting business and when you are not. That allows you a wider latitude of behavior and permits you to be comfortable with traditional values you cherish. For example, I have a friend who is a good role model for this particular problem shared by many women. She's a successful businesswoman and she has a family too. She has learned by trial and error what constitutes effective business behavior. She's perceived by co-workers as firm, competitive, and even aggressive. Her words are matched with compatible nonverbal communications in her dress, mannerisms, and demeanor. However, this woman's behavior in her personal life is another matter entirely. With her husband of many years, she is affectionate and romantic. She even giggles from time to time. Some would see inconsistencies in her behavior and perhaps even label her a phony. She is not. She is a woman who knows what is appropriate business behavior and what is not. And she knows when she is conducting business and when she is not. Once when she and her husband were giving a seminar as part of their work together, he went over to put his arm around her and give her a loving squeeze in front of the participants. She stiffened and glared. The poor guy forgot which woman he was dealing with, the personal one or the professional one. She was clearly the professional woman on that day and he treated her as his wife. He won't do that again. As innocent as it was, his "my little woman" gesture diluted her impact.

Most working women change their image at a crisis point. A personnel administrator's story typifies this. "One day at work I decided once and for all that I was going to stop tinting my hair blond and stop acting cutesy around the men in the office. That decision ended a long-standing internal conflict, a conflict between my conditioning as a traditional woman and my aspirations as a professional woman. For the past four or five months, I have been feeling whole. I act natural now. I am a professional woman who has a private side to her at the same time."

Double Signals

Many women have not come that far. Unknowingly, our appearance and deportment may speak much louder than our words and may be in direct conflict with each other. We may be smiling, amenable cookie givers, our words saying no, you can't have anymore, but our whole bearing saying yes, you can have as many as you want. Unless nonverbal and verbal signals mesh, no adult will be taken seriously. Each of us needs to define the woman we wish to be in order to communicate effectively in business and to be taken seriously. It is much easier to blame the other person—usually a man—for not treating us as professionals when without a doubt a good part of the responsibility for how we are seen belongs to us.

Some women don't consider it a worthwhile day unless at least one person has told them how nice they look or complimented them on their person in some way. It is so important to them that they even goad people into complimenting them. They value themselves only in the area of physical attractiveness and they need constant affirmation because they don't have a good sense of who they are. Others, of course, have developed a sense of self based not solely on packaging but are still encumbered with old mantles that impede their progress such as wearing inappropriate business attire. Harris says that women in her management training workshops who claim to have the most problems on the job are those who do not dress professionally. They're the ones who are sexually harassed more frequently and are generally taken less seriously. (As a note here, I don't care how provocatively a woman may dress on the job, a man is still responsible for his actions if it leads to sexual harassment.) Harris says she hears women say they don't want to dress in what is considered appropriate business wear. "I just want to be myself." "I have a right to be attractive." "I don't want to be neuterized." They opt instead for the plunging necklines and the slit skirts and wonder why they are going nowhere as they continue to send out ambivalent signals and witness their own credibility gap widen.

At the opposite pole is a group of women who have grown up in households where appearances were downplayed. These women are most often described as "dowdy." Even though they may have impressive intellectual credentials, they have not learned even the fundamentals of making a good impression by their appearance. Imagemaker Barbara Blaes says many of her clients in this group come to her out of pain. They feel their careers have suffered because of their appearance.

I suppose deep down it grates on all of us to think that a person is judged on factors other than earned credentials and demonstrated performance. But if we expect justice and fairness at every turn of the road in this world, we are setting ourselves up to be mighty unhappy people. When you hear those in the job market at the executive and consulting levels say that at least 50 percent of the decisions are based on subjective evaluations, then you can begin to see what the right image can do for you. Or what the wrong image can do to you. Blaes says she first became aware of the importance of image at a convention a few years ago. "I noticed that all the men looked professional and the women looked like support staff. One woman in an orange polyester pantsuit (this is not an indictment of orange, polyester or pants, just of this particular suit) got up to give an address and she was well into her speech before I realized she had something important to say. Her appearance had suggested otherwise."

Convey the Message that You Know What You're Doing

Although it may be subconscious, personal considerations such as "How will this person fit in?" are a major factor in the employer's mind. And the employer must consider how other people who are important to the company will view the employee. One top manager thinks the 50 percent figure is far too conservative. He says he has seen times when personal considerations counted for as much as 90 percent of the qualifying factors. With this in mind, you need to pay attention to the image you project. You may not be able to control taxes or inflation, but you can control to a large extent how people perceive you. Management consultant and author Betty Lehan Harragan* says, "In business you are not dressing to express personal

Games Mother Never Taught You by Betty Lehan Harragan, Rawson Wade, New York, 1977. Reprinted with permission.

taste. You are dressing in a costume which should be designed to have an impact on your bosses and teammates. Unless your clothes convey the message that you are competent, able, ambitious, self-confident, reliable and authoritative, nothing you say or do will overcome the negative signals emanating from your apparel." Better yet, executives say a good appearance coupled with an air of confidence can add thousands of dollars to your income.

Of course, there will always be women who object to being told to dress in a certain way. Those who wear the slits and plunges in a business setting will be around for a while, but there will probably be fewer as time goes on. Others say the only thing that matters is their accomplishments and they've made up their minds that they may have to overcome their appearance, but it is a risk they are willing to take. But a third group where the mainstream of women is located is beginning to recognize dress for what it is, a tool to use.

More on Looking Professional

For those who are earnest about acquiring negotiating skills, for those who are aware of the subjective psychological aspects of the employment process, image awareness is a tool. And you should learn to use it. Imagemaker Nancy Ames Thompson describes the impact of image this way: "If you are working, you want to be more important next year than you are this year. One of the best ways to get ahead is to dress like you belong there. Dress so that people can think of you in a higher position. Dress is something you have total control over in moving yourself forward in the business world. You can control the way people look at you and the way they think of you."

You can achieve a professional image without completely dispensing with articles traditionally associated with being feminine. Thompson says you can look professional and still wear colors, jewelry, scarves, nail polish, and other subtle things, but you can't look professional "with a slit up to your navel or with a pushup bra . . . that isn't femininity, that's sex!" As you change your image, it is better to do it gradually so that you will have time to become comfortable with what you are wearing. If you feel ill at ease, others can sometimes detect it, and this destroys the effect you are trying to achieve. Those who are confident are not ill at ease.

A unique aspect of negotiations is that they involve human relationships. You relate to the employer and the employer relates to you. One way to impress is to dress the way ranking professional women in your organization dress—certainly not better or, at least, not flamboyantly so. This can be done even if you are not making a lot of money. By careful shopping you can work on your image. Find out the image of the company before your first interview. Look for clues in periodicals at the library or by talking to friends and acquaintances who may have insights into that organization, or who may know people who work there. If you ever have any question about what to wear, always err on the side of being conservative. Thompson's rule of thumb is "the older the person you are going to see and the more powerful, the more conservative you should dress. Dressing for power is a very conservative thing."

Before you dress you really have to decide, first of all, what it is you are trying to accomplish, how you wish to be perceived, and what's the most effective way to do that.

The Negotiating Outfit

For most women, the skirted suit offers the most advantageous and impressive look for negotiating. Most women do well following this guideline: blazer jacket and matching skirt made from wool, linen, or their synthetic lookalikes in dark, solid colors with a hemline just below the knee. The best colors are medium to dark gray, black, brown, medium to dark blue, dark green, and maroon. However, some women can't wear really dark, powerful colors unless they they add color underneath, for example, a raspberry-colored blouse with a dark blue or black suit. You have to figure out which colors are best for you. The basic business colors, though, are gray, navy, and camel, and one is not particularly more businesslike than the others. Blaes observes that powerful decision makers have always worn dark colors. "If a woman is trying to come across as a power person, the dark colors serve her best. Whereas, if she is in a consulting or similar situation and she doesn't want to intimidate at all, she might go to the beiges, but never to the pastels."

You have more flexibility with the color of blouses than you do with suits, but again, choose conservative styles. The most effective fabrics are cotton, silk, or good quality polyester that resembles cotton or silk.

A briefcase is very much the symbol of a professional woman. It is probably the most readily noticeable thing about a woman's appearance that you can use to label her. The question about purses and brief cases is do you carry both? Perhaps the best answer is to carry a clutch purse which will fit inside your attaché case if you feel you need both. Then the purse can be removed for use if you are going to a luncheon or other function and the brief case can be left behind. I don't think it adds to your appearance to carry one of those big, catch-all purses with who knows what in it. I know a woman who found a jar of maraschino cherries in hers when she cleaned it out.

The shoes to choose are good quality pumps with medium-high heels. A large number of pumps are being sold these days, and I wondered whether this was due to pressure on the industry by professional women. Image consultants I asked scoffed unanimously. The pumps, I am told, are available because of a return to the "forties look." Until now, stores have been surprisingly unresponsive to the businesswoman. Stores are here to make money, and one way they do that is by convincing women of their perpetual need for new clothes that are in style. However, with the entry of budget-conscious women in the work force and also with the tight economy, stores may have to respond to the pressures they are beginning to feel from working women who want clothes to last more than one season. It will be interesting to see to what extent the stores do respond and to what extent women do object to fast-changing trends as opposed to clothing that doesn't go out of style.

A tip on perfume: save it for social events and forgo using it in negotiations. Because the choice of perfume is a personal thing, what smells good to you may not appeal to the person with whom you are negotiating. Or it may be too appealing. Regardless, partly because it is such a personal matter, the use of perfume in negotiations detracts from your professional image.

Jewelry should be kept to a minimum. Basically, tailored gold jewelry goes best with the business image. Wear no more than a watch, a ring, earrings, a pin, or a simple necklace. Avoid anything that looks as if it belongs at a party such as cocktail ring or dangling earrings.

Hair and makeup are, of course, part of your total negotiating look. Extreme makeup and hairstyles can throw off your whole image. As far as hairstyles are concerned, keep away from unusually long or unusually curly styles. They just don't spell business. Use makeup sparingly—mascara, a little foundation perhaps, and lipstick in shades best suited to your complexion. Resist the bright blue or green eyelids. You don't want to look like you've been playing with tester units at cosmetic counters all day.

Don't forget that men are not always up-to-date on the latest items in women's fashions. If a woman is wearing a trendy lip gloss, some men may think, "Why do her lips look so greasy?" Or if a woman wears a fashionable crinkly blouse, they may wonder why her blouse is so wrinkled. This is just one more reason why you should avoid anything too faddish as you put together a negotiating outfit designed to pay off.

After you've given thought to your total look and decided what you're going to wear, focus your mind back where it should be, on strategies to meet your negotiating objectives. Thompson says, "Once you decide upon a negotiating outfit in which you can feel secure in the image you are projecting, you shouldn't have to worry about it again. That security is important because you know what you are saying with your dress, so now you are free to spend your mind time on other things to help you accomplish your goals."

Reduce Self-Defeating Behavior

If you think you are going to feel jittery rather than relaxed, perhaps this perspective will help. Minker says, "Part of being relaxed is getting keyed up. Laurence Olivier is perfectly relaxed when he is performing but at the same time, he is tremendously keyed up. His energy, attention, everything is concentrated on the task at hand. However, if someone misses a cue, he knows how to handle it. He doesn't freeze. He's relaxed."

Irish says you can reduce self-defeating behavior by building on what is real in yourself: "Communicate your accomplishments with conviction, not humbly; be demonstratively agreeable, never appeasing; strong-willed, not willful; conscious of self interests, not dumbly accommodating and be truly open and free with an employer, never disagreeable and hostile." Build on your strengths when you go into a negotiation. Another thing that will help is to consciously center your attention on the other person. By turning your concerns outward instead of inward, you are helping to cure yourself of self-consciousness. Take your attention off yourself and focus it on the other person. How is the employer reacting to my presentation? Are the points I am making hitting home? When you receive positive feedback such as a friendly, affirmative accepting look, then you are on target. Keep on doing what you are doing. When you receive negative feedback, you will have to alter your course until you pick up a positive signal.

Eye contact helps humanize the process and takes some of the built-in hollowness out of it. My establishing eye contact indicates that I am interested in who you are. It indicates that I am not afraid to meet you. If you are asked a question and then drop your eyes as you are about to answer, it suggests that you may be dodging the answer. You aren't trying to hide anything. You are being straight with the employer. Practice good eye contact with everybody you meet so that it will lead to good eye contact in a negotiation. But watch out for too much of a good thing. Who wants to be the object of an intense stare?

Don't slouch or project a laid-back demeanor. Instead, sit up straight and lean slightly forward. This signifies interest in what the other person is saying. A mock negotiation with a friend may help you to identify characteristics that may lessen your impact in a real negotiation. Blinking nervously, especially when discussing important issues, seems to be fairly common in negotiations. Speaking before the other party has fully stated his or her position is another bad habit that should be avoided. One of the harmful aspects of this habit is that the person possessing it seldom reflects on the statements being interrupted. Also along these lines, some people talk too much out of nervousness. Don't feel it is your responsibility to see that every pause is filled. Those who feel that way often reveal entirely too much about themselves. Remember, it is easier to look smart than to sound smart.

Part of your image is made up of how you sound. Your voice informs, persuades, and expresses feelings about yourself and it can add or subtract from the overall bargaining atmosphere. You might want to try speaking into a small cassette recorder in order to identify a voice speed, for example, that may need correcting. When we get nervous, we sometimes talk too fast. And we may catch ourselves using unfortunate phrases like "you know."

Constant fidgeting and a penchant for moving pencils around are other idiosyncracies many are guilty of. Also, if you should read something, hold the notes or paper in such a way that the other person can see the printed words. To hold them up, away from the other person, tends to reflect on your credibility. Do extend your hand when you meet your negotiating partner. Watch for an indication of where to sit and be seated after the employer. Address the employer by his or her title, Mr. or Ms., unless you are asked to use a first name.

Trust Yourself

You don't want to perpetuate the slave-master relationship with the employer, as mentioned earlier. It is not unusual to elevate the other person so far above us that we negate our own self-worth. And the lowering of self-esteem can't help but be reflected in a less positive image and ultimately in poor negotiating results. Irish says, "Start asking questions and evaluate the other person. Feeling subordinate, deferential, grateful (for what, for God's sake?) is the way to qualify for dumb jobs!"

You need to concentrate on achieving something positive in place of only avoiding pitfalls. If you go into a negotiation thinking "I don't know whether this will work or not," or "They are going to give me a hard time and I'm not going to come through well," that's just what will happen. You must feel you have a contribution to make and that you are there with the employer because the employer needs you too. Another mindset that makes it difficult to relax and be at your best is to think of the job as the only place for you in the whole world. Don't think, "This must work out or I'm really going to fall apart." A healthier and more productive viewpoint in negotiations is to think of the great deal you have to offer the company and that if the negotiation doesn't work out, you can go elsewhere. Career consultant Marilyn Shook includes this thought: "The people who interview you are frequently as scared as you are. If you have done your homework well, then you can begin to assist them assist you."

What I am seeking to do is to make you aware of as many elements of negotiating as possible, but I realize that if you feel you have to simultaneously hold all these "dos and don'ts" in your head, you would immobilize yourself in a negotiation. The main thing is to pick up on the areas where you feel you need help and feel free to reject what doesn't apply to you. You know what is best for you. Trust in yourself is a basic component in the image of a good negotiator.

ELEVEN

Negotiating in A Fixed System: Women in Government

What It Means to Negotiate in a Fixed System

She's 32 years old and she's already earning more than $50,000 in her civil service position with the federal government. Sharon Stein, as this woman will be identified, knows what it takes to move rapidly through a fixed system where pay scales are rigidly laid out and she and others like her are eager to share their insights with women who seek to enter and get ahead in government service. With one-sixth of the American workforce employed by government at the federal, state, or local level, negotiating in a fixed system is an important concern. It means making sure you come into the public sector at the highest possible grade and knowing how to escalate once you are in. And there is flexibility in government employment. "Lots of things can be done," says Dr. Ben Burdetsky, a professor of labor and management at George Washington University and a former manager at the U. S. Department of Labor. "There are many old tales floating around which nobody has ever bothered to test."

Stein said about her first job in government as a summer intern while she was in graduate school, "I enjoyed making money so much I decided to stay on in the fall as a research assistant and go to school at night." She attributes her good start to finding a mentor early in her career who told her she could operate successfully in a number of departments if she could gain knowledge about personnel systems, budgets, and procurement.

Change Organizations

Being able to operate successfully in a number of areas is a theme echoed by all the fast trackers I interviewed in government or in private industry. These high achievers don't have one shred of the hangup—loyalty to one organization—that afflicts quite a few women. I have never been sure whether it really is loyalty that holds some women back or whether it is a fear of striking new ground. Of course there are women who have been able to stay in one place and move up through the ranks, but some felt their earnings never caught up with their responsibilities, even though a few had been given raises and promotions without any special effort on their part. They believed the raises and promotions were awarded in order to improve the organization's overall employment picture. For the most part, the women in private industry and government who reach the upper echelons are those who move from job to job.

A high-ranking woman in government told me she had been in four different jobs during her ten years with the government and literally had sent out hundreds of 171s (the official résumé in government). She says, "You cannot be too thin-skinned about being turned down." Sometimes it takes months even to find out if you're on a list of qualified people. The theory is that the more jobs you apply for that are better than the one you have, the more you increase your chances to get a hit. If you concentrate only on one or two places among the hundreds of possibilities, you limit yourself unnecessarily. A job-hiring freeze could come on, the agency you want may be having budgetary problems, or key jobs you think are open may already be slated for others.

Some try only for those positions they feel qualified for over and beyond what is noted in the vacancy announcement, and they don't try for anything that is in a different area or different occupational group. I suppose they feel they wouldn't have a chance at getting hired, but you should pursue other avenues where you have an interest. Don't be put off by the fact that you may not have all the experience and background noted in the applicatiion. As one government employee told me, "Whenever I would find out about a job that I thought would be perfect for me, I would go into the interview and end up not getting it. The best job offers I've received have been when I went into interviews not thinking I had all the qualifications. And these jobs turned out to be far more interesting than I had anticipated."

Job Wirings

Some people don't apply for better jobs in government because they know many of the job openings already are "wired" for a specific person. Job advertisements can be a meaningless formality. The manager knows who he or she wants in that position and has written the job description geared to the favorite candidate's credentials. Conservative estimates place wirings of good jobs in government around the 50 percent level. Others say it is much higher. Even with the realities of this practice in mind, you shouldn't think you are wasting your time by applying. An interview for a higher-paying job gives you a chance to make a new contact in a department or agency, and that manager may have an opening later on that he or she may slate you for. Or the manager may refer you to someone else who has an opening. A third possibility is that the manager will be so impressed with you that he or she may create a job for you. A supervisor told me, "I didn't have a slot for this woman when I interviewed her but after listening to her story and looking at her background, I went in and created a position for her."

Contacts and Sources

Because so many managers in government hire people directly, you should realize that it is not enough just to get your name on one or even several government registers of qualified candidates and wait to be called about a job. You aren't going to be hired in all likelihood sight unseen even if the position in question is not wired for somebody else. There is an enormous difference in reading a résumé and talking to a person face to face. This leads us to another characteristic of the meteoric climbers. They all systematically developed and cultivated a wide cross section of contacts and sources of information. Stein says, "Usually I end up getting a job because somebody has said so and so has recommended you. Can you come in?"

It is good advice to regularly read over a listing of openings. For example, the Federal Research Service, Inc., in Vienna, Virginia, publishes a list every two weeks of roughly 3,500 job vacancies in the federal government. This listing can be found in many federal government personnel offices, college campuses, and libraries, or you can subscribe directly. Whenever possible, go right to the personnel office of the agency where you want to work to see what is available. Do this on a regular basis. Some people haven't had very good luck in dealing with personnel offices but a woman told me she got a GS 14 (a high Civil Service grade) by keeping up a contact in a personnel office. Another possibility is to look through various government manuals and directories to identify high-level officials whose agencies interest you and then write them. Tell them you want to discuss a particular job opening or perhaps future openings. Obviously, if you don't live in the area where the agency is located, you are at a disadvantage. It will require a commitment of time and money in travel logistics, but it may be an investment in yourself that could pay off.

The Women's Network

Women's network groups in government are a growing source of contacts for women. Right now, they tend to benefit women in the lower and middle levels, not the higher jobs, but then most women are in the lower and middle levels. Illustrative of the growth rate of some of these groups, the Women's Transportation Seminar was started in 1977 by fifty women and by 1980 had grown to approximately 300 women throughout the transportation community in Washington.

Many of the tactics discussed earlier for women to position themselves to negotiate for higher-paying jobs in private industry apply equally to women in government. For example, making contacts through various task forces and interagency committees is as effective in government as out of government. Task forces and committees are excellent introductions to other people with whom you may develop working relationships. On committees, people are not observing you strictly on a social basis. They are able to see your work and your ability to get along with other people in a work environment.

Promotion Patterns

If you know people throughout the government system, you will have an advantage finding out information on promotional patterns in various agencies. This will help you to identify those organizations where you can expect to rise quickly. Vickie Pierce of the Environmental Protection Agency says, "I think it is important for people to get a clear idea of what the promotion patterns are within the agency they are dealing with and to sort out what the history has been around people moving in certain grades." You often have to piece together such information as what is the highest grade in any given organizational unit. Where have the people gone in the past year who are in the grade above you? Have they moved along in that unit or have they taken laterals or promotions out of it? All this helps to give you an idea of the opportunities at agencies.

The Department of Transportation's Jane Bachner feels if she had stayed in the same department where she started she would probably be three grades lower because of the stolid promotional patterns there. She urges women to look to the newer agencies, which she thinks have an outlook better suited to upward mobility. Stein also credits much of her success with staying away from the bureaucratic old-line agencies where you might have to go through a more systemized, routinized process. However, another high-ranking woman expresses the opposite opinion. "When I got my GS 14, I got it from the oldest agency in town so I disagree with that." She thinks perhaps your chances are better at some of the old organizations that may have some catching up to do with women workers. But these women aren't looking for special favors. They are looking for organizations where they can use their talents to compete as equals.

Self-Improvement

Another distinguishing quality among those women in the upper ranges was their penchant for self-improvement. One woman went to law school at night not because she wanted to practice law but because the credential of a law degree would further expand her options. Another woman in government said, "I think too many women feel they should get anything, but there are too many other people, particularly males who have the advanced degrees, and I think it is a definite prerequisite for quick advancement." In other words, don't take a course just to take a course. Take courses that will lead to a degree. For those women still in school who are thinking about a career in government, a senior management analyst advises you to get as broad an education as possible to allow you to move into a variety of job series and occupations. She says, and rightfully so, when you are qualified by education to switch from series to series, it permits you greater latitude in trying to get jobs in other organizations. And this educational process should go on once you are in government. Take advantage of the government's tuition assistance programs to further your education.

Pursuing Higher Earnings

The Civil Service Reform Act of 1978 encourages cash awards for outstanding performance in the Federal Government. The awards may now be based on as much as 15 percent of an employee's base salary. Richard Brengel of the Federal Incentive Awards Office says, "This new regard for incentive programs has come about because of more enlightened management. There was a strong congressional and administrative position that incentives were needed to recognize exemplary performance and to motivate persons to improve their performance." In 1979, approximately one out of every eleven employees in the federal government received recognition in the form of a cash or honorary award or a quality increase. A quality step increase, based on excellent performance, provides for an additional one step increase in your pay scale.

Burdetsky observes, "Supervisors by and large do such a poor job (when it comes to giving out incentive awards). They don't have time to think about that aspect." Regarding the quality step increase, "Some managers think about it and use it as a special type of incentive and others probably ignore it because they are busy." Good people who would be awarded a step increase by other managers do not get one under their present manager. Some men and women receive these awards every year and others get them because the manager thinks they should be rewarded for being on the job so long. Burdetsky says he used to review those awards in his department and he could never really distinguish why some people got them and others never did. It is akin in many ways to the performance appraisal. Some managers are tough and they will give you a B. Someone else over there gets an A. That B can reflect performance that is infinitely better than the A because the first manager is a tougher judge.

Considering the high degree of subjectivity that pervades these decisions, are there tactics to help make the decisions go in your favor? Yes. Even in a fixed system, if you put a bigger price on yourself and you do it in an analytical way, you are bound to come out ahead. You can take much the same course in government at this point as what has already been advised for those in private industry. Pursue higher earnings through your performance review and initiate the process with a memo (see Chapter Eight, On-the-Job Negotiating). You have to take the responsibility on yourself. Now that civil service reform is on the books, agencies are having to prepare performance appraisal plans that are being reviewed by the Office of Personnel Management, and these plans have as a necessary element a tie-in with incentive awards.

The Increased Earnings Inquiry

Since the performance review is the most appropriate time for the employee to diplomatically remind the employer how well she is performing, the employee can ask a manager about a quality step increase or a cash award at that review. Much depends on your relationship with your manager. If he or she talks in strong supportive language about the quality of your work, telling you that you have performed in an outstanding way, but offers no indication that any recognition will be forthcoming, then you should follow up with a question at that point. Ask, "Was it your intention to recognize this performance in any formal way?" This is the opportune time for a supervisor to take action. The employee should know ahead of time what the criteria are for a quality step increase or lump sum cash award at her level. You have to have knowledge of regulations to move yourself along. Ask yourself, what is the work I do and what do the regulations say about a person who is doing what I do and doing it satisfactorily? If you know that, it is not a matter of sitting there waiting for someone to notice you.

Another possible route to upgrade yourself in government is by a desk audit through the Office of Personnel Management. Esther Lawton, former Deputy Personnel Director of the Treasury Department and now a management consultant, advises this method only as a last resort but Federal Women's Program Manager Diane Armstrong says requesting one shouldn't create animosity. If you feel the work you are doing is not adequately reflected in your job description, ask your supervisor for a desk audit whereby the work you actually do will be compared against your job description by an appropriate personnel authority. There's a chance that a desk audit could result in an upgrading for you and hence greater earnings.

Negotiating Leverage

Those planning to enter government service might benefit from the experience of a friend of mine who negotiated this way. Her salary in private industry was comparable to the first step of the grade for the job she had been offered in government. By drawing attention to this before she accepted the job, she was able to get her manager to raise her starting salary to the midpoint of the grade range. Depending on what grade you are in, each step increase can vary from $500 to $1,000. And it seems to be standard practice in and out of government that a person should get $2,000–3,000 more in salary each time a job change is made. Although my friend started her career in government several notches above the customary starting point that is the first step of a grade, she isn't to be congratulated. What she didn't demonstrate in the negotiation was that living costs in the city where she had worked were considerably lower than in Washington, one of the most costly cities in the country. In actual purchasing power, she received no increase in earnings at all and possibly took a decrease. My friend was on the right track by negotiating for a higher step in her grade, but she just didn't aim high enough.

If you have an offer to enter the public sector and a bona fide offer of a higher salary from an employer in private industry, use this as leverage to negotiate a higher government entry salary. None of this will be offered to you automatically and it is impossible to negotiate a higher step in your grade after you have begun your duties on your new job.

Like the private workplace, the federal government too wants to know about your previous earnings and requests that you state your salary history on its 171 form, your government résumé. Some people could probably qualify for a Grade 7 but they get hired at a Grade 5 because of previous earnings. Evaluators have been known to assign a grade based on prior earnings regardless of what the qualifications indicated. However, job market analyst Richard Lathrop says he sees some refreshing evidence that the civil service system is getting away from this practice. For example, the federal government is now giving due weight to volunteer experience where there is no prior pay at all. But Lathrop says the fact that pay levels are required on the 171 is negative aspect of the hiring procedure because previous earnings do tend to influence the evaluator charged with determining your entry grade. Since women's earnings are generally on the low side, what is the best way to handle this inquiry? Attach a letter to your completed 171 explaining that the pay level on the form is related only remotely to the quality of work that was being performed. For instance, an applicant from a low-pay area like Florida seeking to qualify for civil service can point out the difference. The applicant can also suggest that the prior earnings level may not be relevant in light of what she has accomplished. As long as the accomplishments are adequately described, the application letter is likely to have some influence.

How to Describe Accomplishments on the 171

How you describe your accomplishments on your 171, as you can see, is an important consideration as you try to negotiate yourself to the highest possible entry grade in government service. Armstrong says, "You can only be evaluated as well as you have described your skills. If you don't describe them adequately or powerfully enough, it may mean a grade or two difference in your initial rating or even determining whether you qualify at all." The federal government requires a description of every job. On the basis of the analysis of that description, the evaluators put a figure on it. But the exact same process is applicable to the negotiating process. You can take a job and describe it easily to fit into the category of a GS 9 and then take that job again and describe it to fit the standards of a GS 12. Both can be accurate descriptions. So why not shoot for the description that will get you a higher grade rather than a lower grade? Burdetsky says, "I don't think most new people coming into government service have any idea of how to fill in a 171 form. When you've been in government service a long time, you know they are very important. How you say it, what you write down, what you consider to be important, the things you emphasize including volunteer service are all important." Management is basically looking for someone who can organize work, assign work effectively, for someone who can initiate, motivate, and evaluate. Lathrop reemphasizes the need to project yourself "in terms of what you can do for the employer. It is terribly important and affects the whole process, not only how well you do but how much pay you get. That applies to civil service as well."

Where to Go for Advice

If you don't know anyone to ask for advice in the government system (federal, state, or local) where you want to work, inquire if there are any women's representatives. For example, the federal government has Federal Women's Program Managers in agencies in Washington as well as in the regional offices around the country. Call the agency where you want to work and get the person's name by asking who is in charge of the Federal Women's Program there.

Armstrong says, "That is one person you can talk to for guidance if you don't know anyone in the government system. It is part of the function of the program." Ask her to read over your application form before you submit it and offer suggestions on how you could improve your chances for a higher evaluation. Some of the Federal Women's Program managers would be the first to admit that they don't have all the answers when it comes to negotiating the civil service arena. You might want to try talking to two or three in various agencies to help you get a better feel for the best way to go about maximizing your potential in skills and earning power.

As a reminder, you can appeal your rating if you believe it is not proper. Information on the appeal process is readily available at Federal Job Information Centers and government personnel offices. Armstrong says, "A lot of people get an ineligible rating and accept it and think that's it, that's the end of it. But you can appeal it to the office that made the decision and there are cases where decisions have been overturned."

Making the Move

If you have professional amibitions and you are thinking about entering government service in the clerical field, don't. There are upward mobility programs that help secretaries make transitions into professional positions, but anybody who has a college degree and who would like to begin a career as program analyst or management analyst, for instance, should turn down offers of nonprofessional positions. That is the carrot traditionally offered to women— enter the secretarial ranks and then make a switch, but that switch is harder than most women think it is. It depends on the agencies, of course, but as a general rule, women should be cautious about entering as secretaries when they know they do not want to be secretaries. Johari Rashad, a Phi Beta Kappa, is now in a professional series in the federal government but she came in as a clerk-typist. "When you choose that route and you know your employer is aware of your background, sometimes you slack up (in your effort to make a transition). You think he or she knows what you can do and they will be looking out for you. That's a mistake. One day it dawns on you that nobody is going to help you but you."

~~&TWELVE&~~

Negotiating
Alternatives

Third-Party Negotiating

Thus far we have discussed only negotiations conducted directly between an employer and an employee. But there are other ways to negotiate. For example, unions select negotiating teams from their membership to bargain collectively for favorable employment terms, and those in the sports and entertainment fields frequently don't negotiate for themselves, preferring instead to go through a third party, or agent.

Negotiating through an agent makes good sense for a number of reasons. For instance, a singer or a writer may have great artistic knowledge but no business acumen to handle complex big-dollar deals. Television news executive Joel Albert says, "If you are moving in high salary circles where paying an agent doesn't hurt, then it makes sense to have one. But if you are competing at the $20,000 level and you are going to give ten or fifteen percent of it away to an agent, then there isn't going to be anything left." Although Albert was referring specifically to television news, agents usually come into play in areas where money-making potential is high such as show business, sports, publishing, television, and the lecture circuit.

Negotiating is only one of the functions of an agent, who often acts as a "body merchant" to help clients find bigger and better jobs or outlets for their talent in addition to working to ensure the success of the current obligations. However, serving as a third-party negotiator is a prime responsibility of agents. Washington-based agent Stan Berk cites the case of Johnny Carson, who doesn't need an agent to find him work but mainly to act as a negotiator. Berk says, "Carson has a nice-guy image to maintain but his agent doesn't. The agent can go in and make the high demands and do the tough negotiating that has to be done." It is a "good guy" versus "bad guy" strategy. Agent Carole Cooper says, "If you don't like something, tell your agent and let the agent do the dirty work . . . . Things can get messy."

Psychological Advantages

The psychological advantages of negotiating through a third party are obvious. You're spared the "mess" but more than this, you are able to preserve an air of being above it all or being somewhat unattainable, which conceivably could enhance your worth to the buyer. Moreover, an agent as a negotiator can say things about you that you might have difficulty saying about yourself. And some of the things that have to be said may be more believable coming from a third party than they would be if you were saying them about yourself. Quite frankly, agents can often press for better deals by virtue of the fact that they have no personal interest at stake except their own financial enrichment. They don't have to worry about facing the other party on a day-to-day basis; their clients do if they negotiate for themselves. Smart agents, however, know they will meet the other person in other business settings and they know how to push just far enough. Broadcast manager Mel Kampmann says, "When agents go for broke to increase the earnings on their commission percentage, they sometimes end up negotiating to the detriment of their clients."

Finding a Reputable Agent

This points up the need to find an agent in your field who is reputable and one you can trust to represent your interests in a style that is most conducive to getting good results without antagonizing the other party to the point of breaking off discussions. Agents with these technical and interpersonal skills are well worth their commissions. But it is hard to find any agent when you are unknown. Agents don't want to waste time on someone who may not make money for them. Author and columnist Art Buchwald says, "For a writer, it is now harder to get an agent than a publisher." That insight led his wife, Ann Buchwald, to become a literary agent. She says if you are looking for a literary agent, get a list of agents and then write to them. You can find such lists in the library. Look in the *Literary Market Place (LMP)*, a standard library reference book. There is also a newly formed Independent Literary Agents Association in New York. Further information along these lines can be obtained from the Authors Guild, Association of American Publishers, and *Publishers Weekly.*

When you write to agents regarding possible representation, be sure to give enough information so that the agent reading the letter can evaluate your concept. As an example of what not to do, Buchwald said she got a letter saying, "I heard you were an agent. I got your name from the Independent Literary Agents Association. I'm looking for one. Would you care to represent me?"

Don't feel you absolutely must have an agent. I didn't when I sent a proposal for this book to about a dozen publishers. When I got several offers from publishers from the mailing, I retained an agent to act as my third-party negotiator. In a creative endeavor that is seen as having good market potential, it is clearly a better strategy to go through a third party for reasons already discussed. That doesn't mean you don't have input into the negotiation. You do. The agent can't agree to anything without your concurrence.

Ask Around

Professionals such as writers, television personalities, models, actresses, and artists of all kinds have peers they can call on to help find an agent or to check out the reputation of an agent. You don't even have to know this person personally before calling. Most people are willing to share this information. Agent Cooper says, "Our business comes from word of mouth and recommendations. We do no advertising whatsoever." If you find an agent in your field who is willing to represent you but you don't know anything about his or her credentials, ask who they have represented and whether they have some present clients you might talk to. A hot market item certainly makes it easier to find good representation.

Getting Rid of a Bad Agent

If you have an agent you feel is doing a disservice to you on a specific project and is not fulfilling a contractual agreement, verbal or written, perhaps you might want to consult an attorney with knowledge of contracts to determine whether you have grounds for a suit to cut or stop payment on the commission. Or if you do get an agent and it doesn't seem to be working out (i.e., you or your product is not making money), call the arrangement off and look for another one. These agreements are usually oral and can be dissolved mutually or otherwise. One of the most successful agents of all times, Irving "Swifty" Lazar, has never had a written contract with a client he represents. Ann Buchwald says the new move in New York is for the agent and client to stick together for one full year to give the relationship time to work for both sides.

Executive Recruiters as Third-Party Negotiators

Unlike agents, the overriding thing to remember about executive recruiters is that they are working for the employer, not for you. Their fees are paid by the employer. Headhunter Eva June says, "My company works for the employer. Therefore, my job is to get the best deal for my client, not the candidate. Nevertheless, we do carry information back and forth between the employer and the candidate on compensation matters and, in effect, become a third party in negotiations." The executive recruiter in salary negotiations is a broker, a middle person, a go-between who can offer the employer certain knowledge about what the salary expectations are for the top job candidates and at the same time tell the candidates what the organization has budgeted for a job.

Executive recruiter Dick Irish says there are times when a recruiter may even try to raise a candidate's aspirations, first because it could mean a higher fee for the headhunter and second because it could mean that the candidate couldn't qualify for the job unless she or he felt capable of earning a higher salary. He says, "The point that headhunters have to keep in mind . . . is the person's ability. Then you talk price." You can have some control in seeing that things develop this way by first communicating ability and putting off the question of money. It is a good negotiating strategy to "slowly develop strength." Job market analyst Dick Lathrop said this about a man he knew: "All the way along the line he had made such an effective presentation of his qualifications that by the time it came to the pay negotiating situation, the employer was talking in much higher terms than the candidate himself thought he could ever qualify for."

Group Negotiating: Women in Unions

Union leaders play key roles in negotiating labor contracts and as more women assume leadership positions in unions, their interest in collective bargaining is increasing proportionately. "We find women in the forefront. They are bargaining and they don't intend to be squeezed out." These words of Betsy Wade, a founding member of a union women's advocacy group called the Coalition of Labor Union Women (CLUW), sum up the attitude of women emerging in leadership roles in labor unions. The traditional role of women in unions—supporting men—is turning around. It used to be true that women wouldn't vote for other women and often women wouldn't run for leadership positions because they believed men could negotiate better contracts. This is changing. If a woman turns down a leadership role today in her union, it is usually because of an overload of family and work commitments and not because she thinks a man could be more productive. Women in unions are now business agents and organizers. And those who aren't may be encouraged to learn about collective bargaining as they observe the performance of women negotiators.

Women labor leaders often find themselves negotiating on two fronts. First, they must convince the male members of the bargaining teams that women's issues must be given proper priority among the issues to be negotiated and then they have to negotiate with management to be sure the issues are written into the contract. Women's increased participation in collective bargaining can be gauged by examining the changes in contract clauses of unions with more than 100,000 members. Over a period of time, there have been more maternity-related provisions put into contracts, along with parental leaves and nondiscrimination clauses. Ann Nelson of the Cornell University State School of Industrial and Labor Relations in New York says, "When you find a nondiscrimination clause in the contract, you know women have been at work." CLUW has a model contract of clauses on women's employment that is available for union women to consult so that they know what issues they can get on the bargaining agenda when contract negotiating time arrives.

One of the main purposes of CLUW, which was founded in 1974, is to increase the participation of women within their own unions. CLUW itself is not a union. It is an organization of women and men unionists, united by their special concerns for women workers yet working within the framework of their own unions. Although the membership in the organization has quadrupled to 12,000, that figure still represents only a small fraction of the 6.5 million women in unions. The recruiting efforts of CLUW are made difficult because membership in unions nationally is declining. Nevertheless, CLUW has 40 chapters around the country; every state has a vice president women can call on for assistance and information. National headquarters are in New York City.

Sources on Collective Bargaining

If you are serious about learning how to negotiate union contracts, there are many sources to help you. A number of workshops and seminars are conducted every year all over the country. CLUW regularly schedules such events. You can probably find one in your area. Many local unions conduct their own workshops and seminars. The AFL-CIO holds collective bargaining workshops at the George Meany Center for Labor Studies in Washington. Cornell University State School of Industrial and Labor Relations sponsors summer workshops at different locations. Such forums are not expensive. The main problem is getting back and forth, but some women car pool to cut transportation expenses. You can keep abreast of these events by referring to your local and national union publications and by attending membership and CLUW meetings. Books on collective bargaining are available in libraries. CLUW has one that costs about a dollar. Also, courses on collective bargaining can be found at many community colleges, universities, and state colleges.

For women in unions, "It is essential that women run for and get elected to bargaining committees so their points of view are represented," says Patsy Fryman of the Communication Workers of America. Some women will encounter animosity from other collective bargainers, but when you are moving ahead, animosity comes with the territory. Wade, who holds offices in the Newspaper Guild, says, "The first time you stand up to open your mouth is the hardest. Nothing is as hard after that."

❧ ENDNOTE ☙

The unexpected benefit in learning to negotiate in the job market is that you will be able to transfer your negotiating skills to other situations. Negotiating is an art that is not tied to gender or one that requires military tactics. Negotiating is simply an awareness that you can have some control over the amount of money you earn, but it goes further than this. Now that the mystery of the art is gone, I've been able to apply its principles and techniques in a wide assortment of ways. My negotiating skills helped me assume more control over my life in general.

I was standing next to a man who began complaining about how much we are at the mercy of car companies. We were at the service department of a local auto dealer where we were both returning our cars because of faulty repairs. As we waited our turns with the service manager, the man continued his monologue. "You know, we are helpless. They have us over a barrel. They know we have to have our cars and they don't care how inconvenienced we are. We have no choice but to accept their terms." I got the feeling it wouldn't have mattered where we had been, he would have found a way to blame his apparently luckless life on the other person, never realizing the real culprit was living in his own mind.

As a negotiator, I accepted none of his conclusions. I was busy sizing up the situation from the other person's viewpoint. I knew most of the jobs at the dealership were endangered because of plunging auto sales and there would be no logical reason why they would deliberately alienate responsible customers. My goal was not difficult to arrive at—I didn't want to be inconvenienced. I decided the best strategy to achieve that was to act as though it had already been determined that I would get a car to use while mine was being worked on. By applying negotiating principles and techniques, including not negating my own power, I left that shop with a new car. As I pulled out of the parking lot, I spotted the man, who had been standing next to me a few minutes earlier, across the street preparing to board a bus. I then turned into the mainstream of traffic and began to pick up speed.

Negotiating Vignettes

The following short vignettes distinguish negotiations from self-defeating exchanges. They are a good way to illustrate that negotiating is something you can learn, or better yet, something you can't afford not to learn. In these brief scenarios, the jobs and the salaries in question are irrelevant. What is important is to apply negotiating tactics no matter what the position. Look to see how the imaginary employee applies many of the techniques discussed earlier. The salaries are not intended to represent any cross-sectional earning pattern among women. As before, I have purposefully used higher figures to help many women realize their greater earning potential.

Exchange Between Cheryl Wilson, a Banking Executive, and Her Prospective Employer

The Wrong Way to Negotiate

Employer   You know, of course, if you join our ranks, you will become one of the few women in the city to hold a vice presidential title.

Cheryl	It's a great honor and I'm thrilled to be considered for the position.
Employer	From what you've told me, your current salary is $26,000. We would be able to pay you $28,500 if you make the decision to come here.
Cheryl	I had expected to make more but it is more than I am making now plus the prospect of being a vice president. I guess your figure is acceptable to me.

A Better Way to Negotiate

Employer	You know, of course, if you join our ranks, you will become one of the few women in the city to hold a vice presidential title.
Cheryl	The title is tempting, indeed, but I would expect to be earning $37,000 before I would leave my current position.
Employer	(aghast) That's 15 or 20 percent higher than our range for the job. $37,000 is out of the question. I'll discuss a salary with you but it won't be $37,000. I can't give you an increase that high.
Cheryl	I'm glad to hear we are at least talking about an increase and I hope we can reach a figure that is satisfactory to both of us. I understood that the $37,000 figure is what others with similar responsibilities are earning here.
Employer	The others have had more managerial experience at a higher level and over a longer period than

you. And besides, you will be new here. Several of the others at your level have worked themselves up through our ranks. It wouldn't be fair to them.

Cheryl   It is my understanding that your main objection to my price is my level of experience and my length of service in the banking field. Is that correct?

Employer   *(Nods in agreement)*

Cheryl   I appreciate the points you have raised, but my contributions are special and frequently unique in local banking circles. I am the first woman to hold an office in the state banking association. I have held management positions in banking for the past nine years. My experience is comparable to or exceeds that of most men and almost all women. I have good working relations with my peers in the community and would not be an unknown quantity joining your organization. If you can't afford $37,000 right away, what can you afford?

Employer   I had set a ceiling for your position at $30,000 but maybe I can swing $32,000. Would that be acceptable? It is quite a bit more than you are making now, isn't it?

Cheryl   My financial package now is in the neighborhood of $30,000, and I am expecting a raise soon. While I am certainly interested in working for your organization, I really don't see how I can accept a salary of less than $35,000. We're only a little more than $50 a week apart. Why don't we give it a try?

Employer   But the $32,000 includes a good package of fringe benefits which will make up a hefty portion of your compensation.

Cheryl   Would you pay the difference that separates us at the end of six months when my performance has been reviewed satisfactorily?

Employer   I think we can agree to that.

Cheryl   I'd like a couple of days to think over what we have discussed here. Perhaps I could come back Thursday afternoon to tell you my decision.

Employer   How about 2 o'clock?

Cheryl   Fine.

Exchange Between Renata Garcia, A Data-Processing Manager, and Her Prospective Employer

The Wrong Way to Negotiate

Employer   What salary level are you looking for?

Renata   I'm making $14,000 now.

Employer   That fits right in with our budget. We are planning to pay $16,000. Is that acceptable?

Renata   I had expected to make more but I do want the job, so I'll take your offer.

A Better Way to Negotiate

Employer	We might be able to work out something with you if we can agree on the salary.
Renata	*(smiling)* I make it a policy never to discuss salary unless I am asked to consider a specific job offer. I'm sure you understand.
Employer	I think we can agree that it is a firm offer if, as I said, we can come to terms on salary.
Renata	Before we get into the area of salary, I am interested in knowing more about your operation. Tell me about plans you have for this department . . . what are some of the goals you hope to achieve?
Employer	The main thing we are seeking to accomplish this year is to centralize our filing system at this location. We will be utilizing the latest technology on the market in computer systems.
Renata	And how would my role fit in with your objectives?
Employer	We need someone who has had experience with a massive computer filing system and knows the ins and outs of such a complicated assignment. In your current job, I understand you have set up a system with 22,000 names . . . that number is in line with our own objective of some 30,000 names. A smooth operation in this area will help improve efficiency in the entire company.
Renata	The challenge sounds exciting and one that I

would like to undertake. What kind of salary range do you have in mind?

Employer Our budget will stand a range from the lower twenties to the lower thirties, but since you lack an MBA, I think we would have to look toward the lower part of the scale as an entrance level.

Renata Lower twenties?

Employer What are you earning at your present job?

Renata My financial package is around $20,000 and I expect both a raise and promotion soon. My employers realize that my salary is lower than it should be and they are trying to catch up. They have told me that I am worth $25,000 but they can't afford to pay that much. Therefore, I am considering other opportunities although I do like my job and the people. The commute is short. In order to make it worthwhile for me to take a job downtown where expenses are higher, I would expect $25,000.

Employer $25,000 is a sizable jump over what you're making.

Renata According to the responsibilities I carry out, $25,000 is representative of my worth. That figure is in line with what others are making on the job market with my qualifications. Some men are getting $34,000. They are frequently paid more than women in this field and I am looking for employment where the pay structure is fair.

Employer But you haven't completed your MBA.

Renata I expect to be awarded my MBA next year but the overriding consideration seems to be that I have five years of data-processing experience which exactly meets your requirements. That knowledge could be immediately transferred to your company with absolutely no on-the-job training. Also, there are no moving or relocation expenses.

Employer   Well, I had $21,000 or $22,000 in mind for a starting salary. I'll have to discuss your request with some of our personnel people. I'll get back to you later in the week.

Renata   I know it is a difficult situation for you to handle and I appreciate your efforts. Perhaps we could meet again on Thursday at 2:30?

Employer   I'll see you then.

The Next Day

Employer   *(via phone)* Would it be acceptable to you if we started you at $22,000 with the understanding that you will be raised to your expectations after a six-month period?

Renata   That sounds workable and fair. I'll give you my answer at our meeting on Thursday.

Exchange Between Sally Kessler, an Administrative Assistant, and Her Current Employer

The Wrong Way to Negotiate

Sally   Gas prices are out of this world. My rent has gone up and I feel I need a raise to make ends meet.

Employer	Sally, I would like to give you a raise, but our budget just won't permit it at this time of year . . . you know that.
Sally	I figured that would probably be the case but I thought I would ask anyway.

A Better Way to Negotiate

Sally	In the eight months since my last review, I've essentially taken on an additional job. When Bill Davis left, most of his duties were turned over to me. While the challenge has been rewarding to me, I should be compensated for the extra work.
Employer	Sally, I am proud of your professional contributions to our firm. We all are. But there is no money in our budget for raises at this time of year.
Sally	The company recorded a 27 percent increase in profits this year. My work contributed to that increase. A raise for me at this time is fair and it is just part of the normal cost of doing business.
Employer	Even if I could give you the raise you deserve, you know it's company policy not to allot raises until annual review time. That's four months away.
Sally	You mean no changes can be made, not even in an emergency?
Employer	Well, the policy can be altered for special purposes, but Sally, your case is not an emergency.

Sally	It is a special case when an employee is not being paid according to her contribution. My workload has increased 50 percent. I have undertaken the added responsibilities with enthusiasm and with success. And I know the company wants to be fair.
Employer	Others in the organization are doing more than their share and they aren't asking for raises now.
Sally	We have a fine group here but I am the only one who assumed the extra duties I now execute over and beyond my job description. And to further assure that I will meet the standards of my new assignment, I have enrolled in two night courses for this fall and winter.
Employer	You are making good points and I am pleased with your accomplishments. Let me discuss this with our personnel department to see what we can do.

Three Weeks Later

Employer	Sally, I am pleased to tell you that your contributions have been carefully evaluated and we have concluded that you have earned a raise and a promotion to Special Assistant to the Director to reflect your increased responsibilities. This reclassification of your job title allows us to give you a $1,500 raise retroactive to the first of this month. Four months from now, you will still be eligible for an annual increase. How do you feel about it?
Sally	I am pleased with your recognition and I do appreciate your confidence in me. Thank you.

Resources to Help You Know Your Worth

Libraries, a Major Source of Salary Data

What You Can Expect to Find and How to Find It

The most readily available current salary information is usually found in periodicals, especially those published by the society or association preeminent in the field. The directories described here are guides to such organizations and their publications.

Directories

Encyclopedia of Associations. Detroit, MI: Gale Research Company. 14th ed., 1980. 3 vols. Vol. 1, *National Organizations of the United States;* Vol. 2, *Geographic and Executive Index;* Vol. 3, *New Associations and Projects* (periodical supplement).
Provides detailed descriptions of over 14,000 organizations including location, size, objectives, publications, dates, and locations of annual convention or meeting. Arranged in 17 broad categories with title, key word, and subject indexes.

The Standard Periodical Directory. New York: Oxbridge Communications, Inc. Biennial. 6th ed., 1978-80.
Information on more than 65,000 United States and Canadian

publications. Entries are grouped in 230 subject areas with cross-references and an alphabetical title index. Each entry includes publisher's address and a brief note on editorial content and scope. The "Employment" section lists nearly 500 periodicals, including publications of federal and state governments on wages and salaries.

Ulrich's International Periodicals Directory. New York: R. R. Bowker, Company. 18th ed., 1979-80.
Worldwide coverage on 62,000 periodicals grouped under 256 subject headings with cross-references. Each entry includes address of publisher, frequency of publication, and indexing information. In addition to periodicals listed under specific subject fields, the section "Occupations and Careers" lists over 80 periodicals of interest to job seekers in any field.

Indexes

These indexes, which serve as a key to periodical contents, should be studied carefully. Information may not appear under the heading you expect, so spend extra time checking other possible headings and become familiar with subheadings and their arrangement. Annual salary surveys relating to a single field can be difficult to locate, but they frequently are summarized in professional or trade journals of the field and can be found through the appropriate index.

Business Periodicals Index. New York: H. W. Wilson Company.
(Monthly except August, with semiannual and annual cumulations.) A subject index to over 270 English-language business periodicals. More than twenty three subject fields are covered, including accounting, advertising, public relations, banking, communications, economics, marketing, printing, and publishing, as well as specific businesses, industries, and trades. Under the heading "Wages and Salaries" are also references to specific occupations, for example, "Accountants—Salaries, fees, etc.," "Advertising agencies—Em-

ployees—Salaries, pensions, etc.," "Personnel managers—Salaries, pensions, etc."

The Magazine Index. Los Altos, CA: Information Access Corporation. (monthly with continuous cumulation.)
This computer-based subject index to more than 370 magazines is published in microfilm only, with each month's additions cumulated into the existing index so that only the current index needs to be searched. The heading "Wages" includes subheadings such as "Wages—Advances," "Wages—Clerks," "--Government employees," "--Surveys."

Public Affairs Information Service Bulletin. New York: Public Affairs Information Service, Inc. (Semimonthly with annual cumulations.)
The *PAIS Bulletin* is an index to periodicals, books, pamphlets, federal, state, and local government documents covering economics, business, finance, banking, public administration, and other fields. There is a computer-based version which may be searched online via the Lockheed DIALOG system (see below). The heading "Wages and salaries" refers readers to additional subjects and to articles under subheadings like "Bank employees," "Executives," "White collar employees," and "Women executives."

Readers' Guide to Periodical Literature. New York: H. W. Wilson Company. (Semimonthly except February, July, August, when it is published monthly. Quarterly and annual cumulations.)
Subject and author index to about 180 popular general-interest magazines. Uses the same headings as *Business Periodicals Index* (see above), but is less business oriented in coverage. The most widely available periodical index.

U. S. Office of Personnel Management. Library. *Personnel Literature.* Washington, D. C.: Government Printing Office. (Monthly.)
Lists material received in the Library in the field of personnel administration. Each entry includes author, title, and facts of publication. Periodicals, monographs, and government publica-

tions are included in a subject arrangement. Prior to January 1979 this was issued by U. S. Civil Service Commission.

———. *Personnel Literature Index.* Washington, D. C.: Government Printing Office. (Annual.)
Excellent index with specific subject headings and numerous cross-references. Material can be found under "Women executives—Pay," "Women engineers—Pay," "Professional employees—Pay," and so on.

Government Surveys

Government salaries—federal, state, county, or municipal—frequently are based on a survey of salaries paid for comparable work in the private sector. Though the survey itself may not be readily available, a look at current city, county, or state pay scales should provide a clue to median salaries private industry pays for the same work. Government pay scales are public information and may be consulted in libraries or personnel or civil service offices.

U. S. Department of Labor. Bureau of Labor Statistics. *Area Wage Surveys.* Washington, D. C.: Government Printing Office. (Annual.)
Under this program the Bureau surveys businesses in 75 metropolitan areas and publishes a separate report on each area. Especially useful for positions in electronic data processing, clerical, and secretarial work. In each category median and mean salaries are reported. Good for local area salary information, but adjustment must be made for time elapsed since collection of data.

———. Bureau of Labor Statistics. *National Survey of Professional, Administrative, Technical, and Clerical Pay.* Washington, D. C.: Government Printing Office. (Annual.)
Summarizes the data collected in the Bureau's annual nation-wide salary survey of selected occupations in private inudstry. Used to

provide the basis for setting federal white-collar salaries. The lag between data collection and publication requires adjustment for inflation and changes in the labor market. Data are often two years old by the time the *Survey* is distributed.

————. Office of the Secretary. Women's Bureau. *The Earnings Gap between Men and Women.* Washington, D. C.: Government Printing Office, 1979.
Based on 1977 data gathered by the Census Bureau, comparisons are made of earnings of male and female workers in 40 occupations, including accountants, computer specialists, health workers, teachers, engineering technicians, managers and administrators, sales and clerical workers. The report lists median earnings for both groups. Figures supplied by The National Science Foundation give comparative earnings for men and women in eight scientific fields using 1976 data.

Special Surveys and Sources

As a reminder again, salary surveys outdate themselves rapidly during eras of high inflation. A survey released in 1980, for example, may be based on year-old data. You will want to make a cost-of-living adjustment yourself on the surveys so that they will more accurately reflect the market's going rate . . . perhaps 8 percent for each year since the survey was conducted. To reemphasize, it is important to look at several sources of salary information in order to get a close and true assessment of your market worth.

Bank Administration Institute. Personnel Administration Commission. *Bank Officer Salaries, A Biennial Survey.* Park Ridge, IL: Bank Administration Institute, 1977.
This report provides minimum and maximum salary ranges as well as current base annual salary. The data are reported by bank size, geographic area and officer classification. For larger banks (resources over $50 million), 34 positions were surveyed. Seventeen

positions were included for smaller banks. Though dated, this is a comprehensive survey for the field.

Endicott, Frank S. *The Endicott Report: Trends in the Employment of College and University Graduates in Business and Industry.* Evanston, IL: Northwestern University. (Annual.)
Prepared with the cooperation of personnel managers in 170 of the nation's larger corporations, the report issued in December 1979 gives their estimates of personnel needs and salaries to be offered to June 1980 graduates. For holders of BA degrees, the survey covers nine subject fields (engineering, accounting, sales/marketing, etc.) with estimates of the number of graduates to be hired at various salary levels in each and the average starting salary. Similar information is given for graduates with BAs or MBAs. Data on salary increases during the first year of work and on average monthly salary of graduates employed five and ten years previously are also given.

American Chemical Society. "Report on chemists' salaries." (Annual.) 1155 16th St. N.W., Washington, D.C. 20036
Salary data reported from a survey of members, including detail by degree status, type of employer, sex, work activity, field and region. Reported in *Chemical and Engineering News*, Vol. 57, June 25, 1979, pp. 39-42.

"Weber Survey on Data Processing Positions," prepared by A. S. Hansen, Inc. (Annual.) 1080 Green Bay Rd., Lake Bluff, IL. 60044
Summarized in *Computer World*, December 10, 1979.

Colleges and Universities

Colleges and universities are important sources of salary information. Surveys of various fields are often found in institutions' career planning and placement offices or respective schools, that is, business, law, education, and so on. You aren't expected to have any difficulty reviewing the material if it is available. Listed here are a number of salary surveys you might find on a college or university campus.

Administrative Compensation Survey Research Report. Published yearly. Compiled by F. Stephen Malott, Frank Mensel, and Jeannie T. Royer. Published by the College and University Personnel Association. Suite 650, One Dupont Circle, Washington, D. C. 20036.
This publication lists the average salaries of personnel at the college and university level in institutions throughout the country. Comparisons are made among school budgets and figures are broken down for both the two-year and four-year institutions.

ASPA Salary Survey. Published yearly. American Society for Personnel Administrators, 19 Church Street, Berea, OH 44017.
The salaries of the following areas are covered in this survey: law, communications/public relations, engineering, history/education/ political science, economics, sociology/psychology, business administration, and personnel/industrial relations. Also includes salaries according to degree (bachelor's, master's, or doctorate).

National Association for Law Placement. Published yearly. National Association for Law Placement. Dickinson Law School, Carlisle, PA 17013
Can be found in most law schools. Does not contain information on paralegal positions. Salary listings for those pursuing a career as lawyers.

CPC Salary Survey. Published yearly with updated information added at intervals during the year. College Placement Council, Inc., P. O. Box 2263, Bethlehem, PA 18001.
Lists entry-level salaries for those with bachelor's master's, and doctoral degrees. Can be found in college placement offices.

State Salary Survey. Published yearly. Office of Personnal Management, Bureau of Intergovernmental Personnel Programs, 1900

E Street, N. W., Washington, D. C. 20415.
Salary information covers 31 occupational categories with 104 titles in administrative, technical, and professional jobs. Data based on level of experience and length of service.

The Following Four Salary Surveys Are Conducted by the Engineers Joint Council, 345 East 47 Street, New York, N Y 10017.

Engineers' Salaries. Special Industry Report. Published every even year (i.e., 1980, 1982).
Found in most engineering schools. Contains data for those entering the field and for those with experience.

Professional Income of Engineers. Published every even year.
Also may be found in engineering schools. Contains data for those entering the field and for those with experience.

Salaries of Engineers in Education. Special Report. Published every even year.
Found in many engineering schools. Contains data for those entering the field and for those with expereince.

Salaries of Engineering Technicians and Technologists. Published in years ending with an odd number (i.e., 1979, 1981).
Contains information on salaries for those entering the field as well as for those with experience.

The Following Three Salary Surveys Are Conducted by the Office of Manpower Studies, American Chemical Society, 1155 16 Street, N. W., Washington, D. C. 20036.

Professional in Chemistry. Published annually.

Starting Salaries and Employment Status of Chemistry and Chemical Engineering Graduates. Published annually.

Report of Chemists' Salaries and Employment Status. Published annually.

Salaries and Attendant Problems of Public Sector Environmental Employment. One-time only publication, 1979. National Field Research Center, Inc., 1522 K Street, N. W., Washington, D. C. 20006.

The Endicott Report: Trends in the Employment of College and University Graduates in Business and Industry. Published yearly. Northwestern University, Evanston, IL. Prepared with the co-operation of personnel managers in 170 of the nation's larger corporations.

The report issued in December gives estimates of personnel needs and salaries to be offered to June graduates. For holders of BA degrees, the survey covers nine subject fields (engineering, accounting, sales/marketing, etc.). Estimates the number of graduates to be hired at various salary levels in each field and what the average starting salary will be. Similar information is given for graduates with MAs and MBAs. Data on salary increases during the first year of work and on average monthly salary of graduates employed five and ten years earlier are also given. (Other fields covered in the survey are liberal arts, business administration, finance/economics, mathematics/statistics, and chemistry.)

Placement Recruitment Exchange, "College Update." Published by University Communications, Inc., P. O. Box 1234, Rahway, N J 07065 Vol. 9, No. 1, October, 1979.

Lists salary ranges for occupations offering employment to business, engineering and other graduates.

American Management Association Salary Surveys. Published yearly. American Management Association, 135 W. 50 Street, New York, N Y 10020.

Salary data on those in top management, middle management, supervisory positions, office and clerical positions, technicians with two-year degrees, and various professional and scientific fields. Many businesses and colleges subscribe to the publications. For those in the office and clerical fields, many junior colleges and secretarial schools have the data from AMA available.

General Publications as a Source of Salary Information

Vocational Guidance Quarterly. Can be found in college placement offices. Periodic articles on women and salaries in various fields. Also found in libraries.

The Conference Board Record. Published by the Conference Board, Inc., 845 Third Avenue, New York, N Y. 10022. Periodic articles on salaries in various fields.

The Occupational Outlook Quarterly. U. S. Department of Labor, Bureau of Labor Statistics. Each publication offers salary information about several occupations.

Bibliography

Otomar J. Bartos, *Process and Outcome of Negotiations.* Columbia University Press, New York, 1974.

Caroline Bird, *Everything a Woman Needs to Know to Get Paid What She's Worth,* David McKay, New York, 1973.

V. R. Buzzotta, R. E. Lefton, and Manuel Sherberg, *Effective Selling Through Psychology,* Wiley-Interscience, New York, 1972.

Phyllis Chesler and Emily Jane Goodman, *Women, Money and Power,* Bantam, New York, 1977.

Sharie Crain with Phillip T. Drotning, *Taking Stock,* Henery Regnery, Chicago, 1977.

Eli Djeddah, *Moving Up,* Ten Speed Press, Berkeley, Calif., 1971.

Julius East, *Body Language,* M. Evans, New York, 1970.

Janet Zollinger Giele, *Women and the Future,* Free Press, New York, 1978.

Francis Greenburger and Thomas Kiernan, *How to Ask for More and Get It,* Doubleday, New York, 1978.

Mack Hanan, James Cribbin, and Herman Heiser, *Consultative Selling,* American Management Association, New York, 1970.

Betty Lehan Harragan, *Games Mother Never Taught You,* Warner Books, New York, 1977.

Margaret Hennig and Anne Jardim, *The Managerial Woman,* Anchor Press/Doubleday, New York, 1978.

Margaret V. Higginson and Thomas L. Quick, *The Ambitious Woman's Guide to a Successful Career,* Amacom, New York, 1975.

John Ilich, *The Art and Skill of Successful Negotiation,* Prentice-Hall, Englewood Cliffs, N. J., 1973.

Richard K. Irish, *Go Hire Yourself an Employer,* Anchor Press/Doubleday, New York, 1973.

Tom Jackson, *28 Days to a Better Job*, Hawthorn Books, New York, 1977.

Chester L. Karrass, *Give and Take*, Thomas Y. Crowell, New York, 1974.

———, *The Negotiating Game*, Thomas Y. Crowell, New York, 1970.

Richard Lathrop, *Who's Hiring Who*, Ten Speed Press, Berkeley, Calif., 1977.

John T. Molloy, *The Woman's Dress for Success Book*, Follett, Chicago, 1977.

Paula Nelson, *The Joy of Money*, Bantam, New York, 1975.

Ralph G. Nichols and Leonard A. Stevens, *Are You Listening?* McGraw-Hill, New York, 1957.

Gerard I. Nierenberg, *The Art of Negotiating*, Cornerstone Library, New York, 1968.

Letty Cottin Pogrebin, *Getting Yours*, David McKay, New York, 1975.

Andrew H. Souerwine, *Career Strategies,* Amacom, New York, 1978.

Nathaniel Stewart, *The Effective Woman Manager,* Wiley, New York, 1978.

John J. Tarrant, *How to Negotiate a Raise*, Van Nostrand-Reinhold, New York, 1976.

Robert A. Whitney, Thomas Hubin, and John D. Murphy, *The New Psychology of Persuasion and Motivation in Selling*, Prentice-Hall, Englewood Cliffs, N. J., 1965.

✦✦ INDEX ✦✦